AF508842

Lighten up!

DAVI LAGO

YOUR

PROBLEMS

ARE NOT

BIGGER

THAN GOD

Translated by
LAURIE ANNE CARPENTER

mcglobal

CIP-Brasil. Catalogação na publicação
Sindicato Nacional dos Editores de Livros, RJ

L174L

    Lago, Davi
       Lighten up! : your problems are not bigger than God / Davi Lago; tradução Laurie Anne Carpenter. - 1. ed. - São Paulo : Mundo Cristão, 2025.
       160 p.

       ISBN 978-65-5988-309-7

       1. Vida cristã. 2. Saúde mental - Aspectos religiosos - Cristianismo. 3. Emoções - Aspectos religiosos - Cristianismo. 4. Paz de espírito. 5. Fé. I. Título.

24-88728   CDD: 248.4
                               CDU: 27-584

Meri Gleice Rodrigues de Souza - Bibliotecária - CRB-7/6439

Editor
Daniel Faria
Proofreading
Guilherme H. Lorenzetti
Designer
Felipe Marques
Typesetting
Gabrielli Casseta
Collaboration
Ana Luiza Ferreira
Cover
Jonatas Belan

Category: Spirituality
First edition: May 2025

All rights reserved by:
Editora Mundo Cristão
Rua Antônio Carlos Tacconi, 69
São Paulo, SP, Brasil
CEP 04810-020
Phone: 55 11 2127-4147
www.mundocristao.com.br

For Natalia,
my wife,
with all my love

Contents

Preface

When I met with Davi Lago to propose that he write *Lighten Up!*, I challenged him to share what ancient biblical wisdom has to teach us about emotional balance. At that time, I commented on the severe physical and emotional implications brought about by the coronavirus pandemic. Yet the feeling of emotional exhaustion is not exclusive to the post-pandemic period. Far from it. Fatigue has become a silent but impossible-to-ignore protagonist. The dynamics of today's society feed and reinforce a constant sense of inadequacy. We are constantly bombarded with visual and auditory stimuli, and becoming disconnected from them can feel like drug withdrawal.

I shared with Davi that emotionally exhausted young people and adults are crowding clinics in an attempt to rediscover the much-desired balance. Thank God for these health-care professionals who dedicate themselves to helping their patients deal with emotional issues. But we believed that a book written by Davi on the topic of emotional exhaustion would add a pastoral approach from someone accustomed to dealing with young people and adults across Brazil. "Come to me, all of you who are weary and carry heavy burdens, and I will give you rest." The Master emphasized that his burden is "light" (Matthew 11:28-30).

Davi accepted the challenge without hesitation. With his usual mastery, he organized the book into ten chapters filled with reflections contextualized for today's world. It is easy to read yet profound, and can be savored gradually. In it we find the most distilled message of Jesus: we need to learn from the Master, who is gentle and humble in heart, and adopt a new attitude towards daily challenges.

With Davi's help, you are likely to identify changes that you need to make in life. Deciding to change is important, and remember that Jesus's burden is light. Whatever issue you need to deal with, remember that no problem is greater than your God. Davi is one of the greatest talents of his generation. During nearly two decades of pastoral experience, he has faced significant emotional challenges and now shares his insights with you. Our hope is that by the end of reading *Lighten Up!* you will discover the rest you need to replenish your strength and to neutralize physical or emotional fatigue.

RENATO FLEISCHNER
Editora Mundo Cristão

Introduction

Let my soul be at rest again,
for the LORD has been good to me.

PSALM 116:7

The Bible contains countless prayers from people who, though physically and emotionally exhausted, found strength and wisdom in God to move forward. By studying these prayers and the various biblical passages that address themes related to feelings of persistent mental fatigue, we learn at least four elementary lessons.

First, *everyone is subject to emotional, mental, and spiritual afflictions, including Christians.* No one is immune to physical and emotional exhaustion. The elderly, adults and "even youths will become weak and tired, and young men will fall in exhaustion" (Isaiah 40:30). Just as the rain falls on the righteous and the unrighteous, so too does extreme fatigue strike the servants of God. The Bible records prayers of emotionally exhausted people, such as Job (Job 3:26), Moses (Numbers 11:15), Naomi (Ruth 1:20), David (Psalm 42:5), Elijah (1 Kings 19:4), Jonah (Jonah 4:3) and Jeremiah (Jeremiah 20:18). The Lord Jesus told his disciples that his "soul is crushed with grief to the point of death" (Matthew 26:38), having prayed to God: "My Father! If it is possible, let this cup of suffering be taken away from me. Yet I want your will to be done, not mine" (Matthew 26:39). Christians are certainly not immune to emotional setbacks, and Christ himself warned that trials and sorrows are part of the journey (John 16:33).

Second, *it is a grave mistake to attribute all emotional and mental afflictions to demonic action, lack of faith, or personal sin.* The

Bible does acknowledge that Satan can harass and afflict people (Mark 1:23-26), that "it is impossible to please God without faith" (Hebrews 11:6) and that sin causes all kinds of grief, including mental exhaustion (Psalm 31:10). But the causes of the emotional and mental setbacks we face are not limited to these reasons. The Bible reveals that there are several other factors that can drain the human soul, such as lack of wisdom, wrong decisions, catastrophes, persecution, physical illnesses, loss of loved ones, interpersonal conflicts, work overload, social isolation, and many others.

Third, *challenges related to mental health must be treated with spiritual and medical competence and responsibility.* Mental health issues are complex, and therefore we must be prudent and responsible from both a spiritual and medical perspective. This means that prayer for healing and Bible study do not negate the importance of seeking help from doctors and healthcare professionals. Jesus acknowledged that sick people need doctors (Matthew 9:12). The evangelist Luke was a physician (Colossians 4:14). Paul advised Timothy on the importance of medical treatment (1 Timothy 5:23). The Bible is full of positive examples of ancient medicinal treatments (Isaiah1:6; Ezekiel 47:12; Jeremiah 8:22). The responsible treatment of emotional exhaustion and other mental health issues should include medical supervision if necessary.

Fourth, *in Christ, there is wisdom, strength, and hope to achieve emotional and spiritual integrity.* The Bible is very clear in stating that the greatest of all human problems is sin, human disobedience to the will of God the Creator. Because of sin, human beings are deprived of the glory of God (Romans 3:23) and subject to eternal condemnation (Romans 2:6-12). But the Bible teaches that Jesus Christ died on the cross in the place of sinners, bearing the righteous wrath of God upon Himself. Therefore, in Christ, hope is not a mere wish; it is a reality. He himself invites us: "Come to me, all of you who are weary and carry heavy burdens, and I will give you rest" (Matthew 11:28). Jesus not only frees us from sin but also teaches us the way to a wiser and more integral life in all its dimensions, including emotions, thoughts, and relationships. The Scriptures literally teach that all the treasures of wisdom and knowledge are hidden in Christ (Colossians 2:3).

In light of these essential lessons, the purpose of this book is to present a set of practical pastoral guidelines for anyone who wishes to develop emotional, mental, and spiritual integrity.

Prospective studies have found that elements of Christian faith and practice benefit those with psychotic disorders and depression, increase happiness and resilience, and decrease the risk of substance abuse or suicide. Although teaching that over-spiritualizes or discourages timely interaction with health care and consistent treatment concordance is sometimes harmful, the evidence suggests that Christianity is generally a positive influence on mental health.[1]

Thus, I believe that this book can help those facing challenges such as constant sorrow, confused thoughts, and emotional exhaustion, those who want to prevent these issues, and those who want to help others achieve restoration through Christian wisdom.

1

Vent, Lament, and Cry

There are moments when we feel that life's usual frustrations are starting to accumulate. This is especially true when we make a big mistake or when we go through difficult times, such as the loss of a loved one, the end of a romantic relationship, a disappointment, a social upheaval, a serious illness, or a significant financial loss. In this chapter, we will consider three attitudes recommended in the Scriptures for times when our inner life feels completely crushed. They are: venting, lamenting, and crying.

To vent is to reveal the doubts, anxieties, and anguish that torment us from within. When we vent, we acknowledge what is troubling us and share it with someone we trust. Venting is expelling the poison that is destroying our emotional well-being. Scientific studies affirm that the practice of venting is essential for emotional regulation, reducing stress, and strengthening the immune system.[2] Through venting, the afflicted person can calm their mind, better understand their own emotions, and feel understood and accepted. Without venting, we might either explode or implode emotionally. We explode when we become irritable, aggressive, impatient, and mistreat people who have nothing to do with our problems. We implode when our inner life spirals into sad and bitter thoughts, which can even trigger maladies such as ulcers, insomnia, irritable bowel syndrome, panic disorder, and depression. The Bible explicitly teaches: "Watch out that no poisonous root of bitterness grows up to trouble you, corrupting many" (Hebrews 12:15). Bitterness is compared to a toxic plant that begins to develop roots in our lives.

How do you allow yourself to vent? The first step is to recognize the ongoing internal pressure. Problems do not disappear if we simply ignore them. There's no point in lying to ourselves and pretending that everything is fine. In every venting process, we humbly acknowledge, first and foremost, that our inner state is not well. Next, we need to lower our defenses and open our hearts. Some people prefer to write down their thoughts, while others prefer to voice them to someone. The main question is: with whom can we vent?

There's a certain relief in saying things out loud, even if it's just to ourselves. There are people who talk about their problems to pets or even to an object(!). In the 2000 movie *Cast Away*, the protagonist Chuck Noland, played by Tom Hanks, has been alone and stranded on an island for so long that he starts to vent and talk to a volleyball, which he names Wilson. Wilson's "performance" in the film was so notable that it received the 2001 Critics' Choice Award in the curious category of "Best Inanimate Object in a Movie." With advances in technology, "psychotherapist robots" have even emerged—online chat rooms where distressed people talk to automated attendants and artificial intelligence programs.[3]

As the Scriptures indicate, however, confiding in another flesh-and-blood person in whom we trust is of great importance. For example, in Genesis we read that before the creation of woman, Adam felt lonely because there was no one who interacted with him as a human being. God himself stated, "It is not good for the man to be alone" (Genesis 2:18). We find another example at the end of the Third Epistle of John, where the author, after addressing various important instructions to the recipient, states that there were other matters that should be addressed, but not with "pen and ink" (3 John 1:13). There are limits to interactions with non-human entities (such as animals and robots), just as there are limits to human interactions mediated by communication technology. Finding another human being to confide in is very valuable for mental health.

A significant challenge to overcome is the fear that many people have of exposing their vulnerabilities. This fear is understandable. After all, most people are raised from childhood to hide their weaknesses and not to expose their frailties for fear of being stigmatized, ridiculed, viewed negatively, or disliked. Moreover, in the transition to adulthood, we are taught to respect the feelings and space of others. As we mature, we understand that we should not say everything we think all the time and learn to control our reactions, expressions, and responses. So far, so good. The problem occurs when a person is completely overwhelmed in their inner life and begins to feel the weight of these disproportionate emotional burdens on their own. In these circumstances, we need to acknowledge our distress and seek trustworthy people to confide in. Holding onto grievances can make them seem bigger than they actually are. Joy shared is joy doubled; sorrow shared is sorrow halved.

Choosing the best person in whom to confide is a key issue. After all, it is not wise to talk about our anxieties whenever we feel like it with just anyone. There are problems that only get worse if we share them with the wrong people. Thus, it is very common for our confidants to be our family members and loved ones: the husband who opens his heart to his wife or the daughter who opens her heart to her mother. It is in these moments that we also comprehend the great value of our friends. A true friend remains when everyone else disappears. Do not

JOY SHARED

IS JOY DOUBLED,

SORROW SHARED

IS SORROW HALVED.

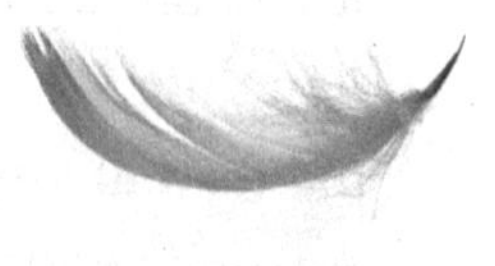

confuse those who are "friendly" with those who are true friends. Beware of false friends: "Many will say they are loyal friends, but who can find one who is truly reliable?" (Proverbs 20:6). Be careful not to unnecessarily expose your intimate anxieties to people who only wish to take advantage of you. True friends are those who have proven over time that they care about you, who listen to your complaints without making quick and hasty judgments. When we confide in true friends, we have the opportunity to deepen relationships, for "a friend is always loyal, and a brother is born to help in time of need" (Proverbs 17:17).

In addition to friends and loved ones, we can also confide in qualified counselors, such as church elders, people of deep faith, and mental health professionals. According to biblical teaching, the church is not merely a backdrop but a vibrant community, a living forum for the deepest issues of life. Thus, Christians are exhorted to "teach and counsel each other" (Colossians 3:16) and "share each other's burdens" (Galatians 6:2).

Yet there are situations in which we feel extremely alone. Talking with other people, or even confiding in animals, robots, or inanimate objects does not satisfy us. Throughout the Bible, we find encouragement to bring our troubles to God. The wisdom of the psalmists declares that "God is our refuge and strength, always ready to help in times of trouble" (Psalm 46:1).

In early 2021, my mother, Esmeralda, was nearly on her deathbed in the intensive care unit of the Felício Rocho Hospital in Belo Horizonte. Infected with COVID-19, she had been on a ventilator for several weeks and was showing no signs of improvement. I was staying at a small hotel across from the hospital and was completely exhausted, unable to sleep properly. My mother was 59 years old at the time, and I was devastated by the prospect of losing her. One night, I read in the Bible Jehoshaphat's prayer to God in his moment of distress: "We do not know what to do, but we are looking to you for help" (2 Chronicles 20:12). I made Jehoshaphat's prayer my own. I poured out my heart to God, expressed my anguish, and unburdened all my anxiety. I immediately felt stronger: it was a moment of renewal in my spiritual life. By God's mercy, my mother's health was restored, and after 94 days in the hospital, she came home.

Even so, the difficult situations we face do not always have positive turnarounds. At this point, it is worth emphasizing the importance of *lamenting*. Lamentation is an act of unequivocal honesty by a person of faith before God, in which they fully express their pain. According to lamentation scholars, biblical lament typically includes four common elements:

1. It is directed to God.
2. It presents a complaint.
3. It makes requests for justice.
4. It reaffirms a commitment of faith and hope in God's promises.[4]

Unlike grumbling, which is sullen complaining, the Scriptures teach that lamentation is the response of a person who is genuinely faithful to God in the face of great sorrows. Grumbling is merely complaining without faith; lamenting is expressing anguish while maintaining faith in God. Thus, grumbling is biblically treated as a sin, whereas lamentation is considered a blessing.

The biblical book of Lamentations is instructive in this regard, as it records songs of anguish from God's people after the devastation of Jerusalem around 586 B.C. Written with stylistic mastery and deep spiritual sensitivity, Lamentations is a poem that leads us to reflect on the place of everything in our lives. For the people of Israel, lamentation incorporated not just words but also actions: "The leaders of beautiful Jerusalem sit on the ground in silence. They are clothed in burlap and throw dust on their heads. The young women of Jerusalem hang their heads in shame" (Lamentations 2:10). Other examples in the Old Testament related to lament include:

- Covering the head (2 Samuel 15:30; Esther 6:12).
- Beating the breast (Isaiah 32:12-13; Jeremiah 31:19).
- Wearing mourning garments (Genesis 37:34; 2 Samuel 3:31; Esther 4:1; Job 1:20; Isaiah 37:1; Jeremiah 41:5).
- Sitting or lying on the ground (2 Samuel 13:31; Job 2:13; Jeremiah 6:26; Lamentations 2:10).
- Fasting (Judges 20:26; 1 Samuel 31:13; 2 Samuel 1:12; 12:21).
- Consuming food and drink during mourning (Jeremiah 16:7; Ezekiel 24:17,22; Hosea 9:4).
- Abstaining from sexual relations (2 Samuel 11:27; 12:22-24).
- Renouncing the use of cosmetics and oils (2 Samuel 12:20; 14:2; Isaiah 61:3).
- Chanting laments and funeral songs (2 Samuel 1:17-27; Amos 5:16-17; Malachi 1:8).

It is edifying for us today to learn about these ancient ways of lamenting. After all, people in modern society have created numerous distractions and ways to hide their pain—from others and from themselves. Others have instrumentalized lamentation as a means to promote scandals, attract media attention, and make money. Yet the absence of genuine lament in our lives can be fatal to mental health. It is wise for us to relearn how to lament. The Christian tradition has much to teach in this regard. We, as Christians, understand that in Christ Jesus, God himself entered into human suffering. On the cross, in particular, the Son of God expressed his pain with a psalm of lament: "My God, my God, why have you abandoned me?" (Matthew 27:46; see Psalm 22:1). In this profound identification of God with human suffering, we find comfort, relief, and new hope.

Scholars assert that the Passion of Christ broke with the ideal of the "noble death," widely disseminated in ancient cultures. This ideal finds its earliest expression in the heroic death, the glorious death in battle, and its more philosophical expression in the death of Socrates.[5] As Plato recorded in his work *Phaedo*, Socrates was condemned to death and faced his fate with placid tranquility: he calmly drank the cup of hemlock that would kill him while his students suffered and cried in sorrow.[6] Jesus, on the other hand, suffered and agonized on the cross. The Christian ideal, therefore, is not emotional resignation, mere stoicism, nor apathy. The Christian ideal of facing pain involves lamenting and weeping. There are things that we can only see through tear-filled eyes.

Jesus himself shed tears. In the Old Testament, prophets weep, priests weep, kings weep, but in the Gospels, the Almighty weeps. Reflecting on the tears of Jesus, the Patristic theologian Origen distinctly used the expression "tears of God."[7] This brings us to the final point of this chapter: the value of *crying*. According to the New Testament records, it is unquestionable that Jesus was happy and good-humored. Yet it is interesting to note that, although it is presumed, the Bible does not explicitly mention even once that Jesus smiled. On the other hand, it is explicitly mentioned at least three times that Jesus wept: the Gospel of John records that Jesus wept at the death of his friend Lazarus (John 11:35); Luke states that Jesus wept over the tragic fate of Jerusalem (Luke 19:41);[8] and Hebrews points out that "while Jesus was here on earth, he offered prayers and pleadings, with a loud cry and tears, to the one who could rescue him from death. And God heard his prayers because of his deep reverence for God" (Hebrews 5:7). In John's text, the Greek term used for weeping indicates silent crying, while the term used in Luke indicates audible weeping,[9] just as tears are associated with loud cries in Hebrews.

These records reveal that Jesus immersed himself in the roots of human misery, identifying with humanity's suffering and weeping in every way. Thus, Christ's tears give dignity to our sorrow and freedom to our emotions. Christ wept and empowers us to weep.

Therefore, do not hold back your tears. Cry. Crying generates a self-soothing effect that alleviates stress and provides a sense of well-being. Scientific evidence indicates that when we cry, our body releases endorphins that relieve tension, similar to the effect of physical exercise.[10] Crying helps stabilize our mood by releasing toxins accumulated from emotional stress.[11] Crying also communicates the need for help, acting as an easily detectable alarm. Various studies have concluded that those who cry receive more attention, are considered more likable, and are helped with a greater sense of connection and companionship.[12] Crying and lamentation also free us emotionally to forgive and pray for those who have offended us. Crying makes us more empathetic. After all, if we do not acknowledge and weep over our own losses and struggles, how can we identify with those who are suffering? How will we be able to "weep with those who weep?" (Romans 12:15).

There is strength in tears. With tear-filled eyes, we see things that, otherwise, we would be unable to notice. Thus, to cleanse our eyes from the world's lies, we need to learn to truly weep. God made us with tear ducts, and there is a time for everything, including a "time to cry" (Ecclesiastes 3:4). The Scriptures illustrate many appropriate occasions for crying:

THERE ARE THINGS
THAT WE CAN ONLY
SEE THROUGH
TEAR-FILLED EYES.

- Tears of sorrow (1 Samuel 30:4; Nehemiah 1:4).
- Tears of mourning (Genesis 23:2; 2 Samuel 1:12; Acts 9:39).
- Tears of farewell (1 Samuel 20:41; Acts 20:37).
- Tears of reunion (Genesis 33:4; 43:30; 46:29).
- Tears of repentance for sin (Matthew 26:75).
- Tears of pleading to God for an answer to prayer (1 Samuel 1:7-8; Isaiah 38:5).
- Tears of surrendering the heart before God (Psalm 6:6; 42.3).

While we are alive, we will go through moments of anguish that will make us lament and cry, but these experiences are temporary (John 16:33; Romans 8:18). Our tears are precious to God. The Bible teaches that the Lord not only sees and knows our tears but collects each one in a jar and records them in a book (Psalm 56:8). In heaven, God will wipe every remaining tear from our eyes (Revelation 21:4). Until that day comes, the ability to cry is a blessing: "God blesses those who mourn, for they will be comforted" (Matthew 5:4).

Hot tears do not flow from cold hearts. If our eyes are dry, perhaps it is because our heart has become a desert. On the other hand, if we are broken, it may be an indication that God is already working in us to make us more like Christ. And the more we resemble Christ, the deeper our humility, the more mature our character, and the more complete our surrender to God.

2

Cultivate the Virtue of Humility

> Humility is the altar upon which God wants us to sacrifice to him.
>
> FRANÇOIS DE LA ROCHEFOUCAULD[1]

omeone once said to me, "Davi, not even Newton understands the gravity of my problems." Indeed, we do not live
in the world we desire, but in the world that exists. Things
do not always go as planned, and from time to time, we are unsure
which path to take. Thus we are weary in the face of challenges. In
a way, living means facing problems. As the poet Paulo Leminski
said, "problems have a big family, and on Sundays, they all go out
for a walk, the problem, his wife, and other smaller problems."[2]
Thousands of years ago the Book of Job decidedly summarized
this human condition: "Is not all human life a struggle?" (Job 7:1).
So the question that many people face is: How do we avoid going
crazy when we face so many problems? How do we deal with the
multiple challenges that life imposes? Where do we start?

Perhaps the most fundamental guidance we can glean from
the treasures of biblical wisdom on caring for our mental, emotional, and spiritual health is to *cultivate the virtue of humility*.
Proverbs states that "pride leads to disgrace, but with humility
comes wisdom" (Proverbs 11:2). This maxim presents two internal attitudes (pride or humility) that can lead to different external outcomes (disgrace or wisdom). The notion of "pride" in
this text comes from a Hebrew word that suggests boiling water
until it rises and spills out of the container, and it applies to the
arrogance of those who demand to have everything according
to their whims.[3]

AS A RULE,
PROUD PEOPLE
DISPLAY ARROGANCE
BRED FROM THEIR OWN
PSYCHOLOGICAL
INSECURITIES.

Proud people do not ask for permission, they just push their way through. They do not apologize when they are wrong; they justify themselves. They do not give explanations when appropriate; they threaten. They never thank; they always demand. They do not pray; they curse. They do not forgive; they seek revenge. They do not praise those who deserve it; they complain about everything and everyone. As a rule, proud people demonstrate arrogance stemming from their own psychological insecurities. Various empirical studies in social psychology identify that individuals who exhibit selfishness and narcissism show higher levels of aggression when they hear insults that threaten their egos.[4] In everyday life, a haughty person only cares about others insofar as they serve their own exaltation. According to Scripture, this is the fundamental error of the proud person: they are closed in on themselves, seeking an illusory "independence."

Pride, therefore, hinders access to wisdom, causing people to harm themselves (Proverbs 8:36) and create unnecessary conflicts with others (Proverbs 13:10). In other words, pride opens the doors to a hellish life, and ruin can literally come from any direction.

At the extreme opposite, "haughtiness goes before destruction; humility precedes honor" (Proverbs 18:12). Unlike pride, humility is the abandonment of the pursuit of independence. A humble attitude indicates an open, understanding, attentive, and modest spirit. The Old Testament describes the humble as those who are not impressed with their own wisdom (Proverbs 3:7), do not boast about the future (Proverbs 27:1), do not seek honors (Proverbs 25:27), and do not praise themselves (Proverbs 27:2). In other words, a humble person does not assume they are better than others or that they have all the answers. They do not try to draw attention to themselves nor strive to appear important. The humble are described as sensible people who listen to good advice and are not stubborn or resistant to necessary changes (Proverbs 15:31-33). Humility is also explicitly associated with the practice of justice and mercy (Micah 6:8).

It is crucial to emphasize that, in the Hebrew understanding, all this wisdom about humility has a theological origin; it is rooted in the belief that only God is perfect. For the people of Israel, humility is directly linked to the fear of God: "Fear of the Lord teaches wisdom; humility precedes honor" (Proverbs 15:33; see also 22:4). Thus, humility can be understood as the virtue of honestly evaluating all things in light of God's perfection and of human limitations—in all their dimensions.

The Christian faith has embraced the Israelite understanding that God opposes the proud and gives grace to the humble (Proverbs 3:34; Luke 1:52; James 4:6; 1 Peter 5:5). In fact, Christian thought placed humility at the center of moral life in a dramatic and unprecedented way. From the Christian perspective, God— precisely because he is perfect—cannot exalt himself above what he is in his Most High Being. But he can humble himself, as he indeed did in Christ Jesus, who

> Though he was God,
> > he did not think of equality with God
> > as something to cling to.
> Instead, he gave up his divine privileges;
> > he took the humble position of a slave
> > and was born as a human being.
> > When he appeared in human form,
> > he humbled himself in obedience to God
> > and died a criminal's death on a cross.
>
> Philippians 2:6-8

The gospel proclaims that Jesus, the Son of God, came to the world to give his life as a ransom for humanity lost to pride and sin. Thus, Christians understand that God revealed himself supremely through his humility. After his humiliation to the point of death on the cross, Jesus was exalted as the conqueror of the world and over death, hell, and sin. This hymn about the humiliation and exaltation of Jesus in Philippians 2 identifies humility both as his defining characteristic and as one that his followers should carefully imitate. Undoubtedly, the Christian emphasis on humility has radically transformed the understanding of what constitutes a successful human life.

In the Gospel of Matthew, Jesus began his most famous discourse, the Sermon on the Mount, with this disconcerting statement: "God blesses those who are poor and realize their need for him, for the Kingdom of Heaven is theirs" (Matthew 5:3). In contrast to his immediate cultural context, which viewed humility as an obstacle to human flourishing, Jesus repeatedly asserted the exact opposite: humility is the path to genuine flourishing. Jesus's invitation was direct: "Take my yoke upon you. Let me teach you, because I am humble and gentle at heart, and you will find rest for your souls" (Matthew 11:29). In other words, peace does not begin within ourselves, but in him. Even more surprisingly, peace begins with learning his humility and gentleness.

Jesus Christ did not invite his disciples to learn how to become rich, perform impressive miracles, or become famous religious priests, but to learn humility of heart. There is something completely new in these words. For example, Augustine of Hippo stated that this perspective on humility "is not found in any book of the Epicureans, the Stoics, the Manicheans, or the Platonists. All of them have excellent precepts about customs and discipline; however, this humility is not found there. The stream of this humility comes from another source: it comes from Christ."[5] It is not surprising that several of the early church theologians considered humility to be the quintessential Christian virtue,[6]

THE CHRISTIAN EMPHASIS ON HUMILTY HAS RADICALLY TRANSFORMED THE UNDERSTANDING OF WHAT CONSTITUTES A SUCCESSFUL HUMAN LIFE.

meaning that all other virtues are built and sustained upon this foundation: the loving humility demonstrated in God's self-revelation in Jesus. Augustine questioned: "did [Christ] teach anything other than this humility?"[7]

Jesus Christ is the ultimate definition of humility. The New Testament presents various characteristics of a humble person, transformed by Jesus:

- Gratitude (1 Thessalonians 5:18).
- Ability to understand and quickly forgive others (Colossians 3:12-14; Ephesians 4:31-32).
- Teachable heart (2 Peter 3:18; 1 Corinthians 4:7; James 3:17).
- Helpful and eager attitude in assisting others (Ephesians 4:29).
- Willingness to serve (Galatians 5:13-14; Matthew 23:11-12).
- Valuing the interests of others (Philippians 2:3-4).
- Respect for all people and honor for the elderly (1 Peter 5:5).
- Friendship with the needy (Romans 12:16).
- Absence of arrogance (Luke 14:11).
- Self-control to avoid retaliating against insults (1 Peter 2:21-23).
- Tolerance in love (Ephesians 4:2).
- Trust in God's grace (2 Corinthians 12:9-10).

In a society where success is defined in terms of productivity and self-sufficiency, humility is mistakenly associated with passivity and low self-esteem. In the modern era, philosophers such as David Hume and Friedrich Nietzsche, for example, railed against the Christian emphasis on humility.[8]

Despite its detractors, however, the Christian notion of humility has endured through the centuries and remains relevant in multiple fields, such as philosophy,[9] psychology, and social sciences.[10] Even the cynical writer La Rochefoucauld acknowledged that "humility is the true test of the Christian virtues; without it we retain all our faults, and they are merely covered by pride, which hides them from people, and often from ourselves."[11]

A humble person is able to see themselves accurately, understanding their talents and flaws, while being free of arrogance and low self-esteem. Humility disarms us of the "Messiah syndrome," which is the illusion that we must face life's problems as if we were capable of saving the world, as if everything depended solely and exclusively on ourselves. On the other hand, humility also disarms us from the feeling of being a "victim of the universe," which is the illusion that it is impossible to do anything to face our challenges. Victim-minded people become fatalistic, inert, and complacent. They are always ready to blame others for everything that goes wrong and constantly shift their responsibilities. Both the Messiah syndrome and the victim complex are two sides of the same coin: pride. Arrogant people might believe they can solve everything on their own or "decree" that nothing can be done. The same arrogance permeates both attitudes. Humility, thank God, frees us from this.

3

Create Cycles of Rest

In the most restless age of history,
Christ can give you rest.

BILLY GRAHAM[1]

We shouldn't need to suffer a physical and emotional collapse to understand our limits. Taking a break from work is vital because our energy is finite. The human body needs to breathe, sleep, be hydrated, and be nourished.

Despite the fundamental nature of rest for human life, however, multitudes of people around the world suffer from exhaustion. A study by the Oswaldo Cruz Foundation ascertained that 72% of Brazilians have sleep disturbances, such as insomnia.[2] Unfortunately, there is a growing number of workers diagnosed with the so-called *burnout syndrome* or *professional exhaustion syndrome*. This syndrome is defined as an emotional disorder with symptoms of extreme exhaustion, stress, and physical depletion resulting from draining work situations.[3] The World Health Organization does not consider burnout syndrome a disease per se, but in 2022 it designated it as an "occupational phenomenon," and highlighted the need to focus on it for improved health in the professional context.[4] Professional exhaustion or burnout is understood as a process in time and a vicious cycle which includes three dimensions:

- Emotional exhaustion: refers to feelings of being depleted of one's emotional and physical resources.
- Cynicism or depersonalization: represents the interpersonal context dimension of burnout.

- Reduced personal accomplishment: refers to feelings of incompetence and a lack of achievement and productivity at work.[5]

The main identified cause of burnout is excessive work. Experts worldwide unanimously recommend that the best way to prevent burnout is to learn to live a balanced life and reduce work-related stress. In this context, it is remarkable that the Bible, from its very first page, emphasizes the importance of balance between work and rest. God Himself, after creating the world in six days, rested on the seventh day, the Sabbath, and blessed and sanctified it (Genesis 2:1-3). The Hebrew word *shabbath* means to rest, cease, or stop working. Later, after liberating the people of Israel from slavery in Egypt, God established the fourth commandment of the Decalogue:

> Remember to observe the Sabbath day by keeping it holy. You have six days each week for your ordinary work, but the seventh day is a Sabbath day of rest dedicated to the Lord your God. On that day no one in your household may do any work. This includes you, your sons and daughters, your male and female servants, your livestock, and any foreigners living among you. For in six days the Lord made the heavens, the earth, the sea, and everything in them; but on the seventh day he rested. That is why the Lord blessed the Sabbath day and set it apart as holy.
>
> Exodus 20:8-11

Although there are various biblical elaborations on the Sabbath principle of rest, our focus in this chapter will be on four specific aspects: the divine origin of rest, the limitation of work, the importance of cycles of rest, and the act of sleeping with faith.

First, the Sabbath principle teaches that *rest begins with God*. Today, many see rest as a reward to be earned after work. But the Bible states the opposite: rest did not come at the end, but at the beginning of human life. In Genesis, God created humanity on the sixth day of creation, and on the seventh day, he rested. Notice that humanity's first full day was a Sabbath, a day of rest, a blessed and sanctified day. Rest is the foundation of human life, not its conclusion. Rest was the starting point from which all human work would commence. Thus, the Bible teaches that the rhythm of life established by God includes working from a place of rest and sanctification. Everything begins in communion with the Creator.

In this sense, rest is, above all, a spiritual theme, relating to our relationship with God. The Letter to the Hebrews teaches that Jesus Christ is the true Sabbath and our rest (Hebrews 4:1-16). The Lord Jesus Himself said, "Come to me, all of you who are weary and carry heavy burdens, and I will give you rest" (Matthew 11:28). Jesus did not tell us to go to a priest, a pastor, or any other direction, but to Himself: "Come to me." He invites us to Himself and offers a unique rest: "and you will find rest for your souls" (Matthew 11:29). Many people have expensive beds and fine linens but do not have blessed nights of sleep because they live with a conscience burdened by guilt and sins. Only Jesus can purify our soul. Biblically, the deepest dimension of rest is spiritual and begins when the grace of Christ reaches and transforms us

Second, the Sabbath principle establishes the importance of *placing limits on work*. When God instituted rest on the Sabbath, the Israelites recognized the stark contrast with their enslaved lives and the frantic work pace they endured in Egypt under Pharaoh's oppression. Establishing a limit on work, therefore, is an act of faith and obedience to God, and a resistance to a materialistic view that reduces human life to producing and consuming goods. Work must have boundaries in time, space,

THE FIRST FULL DAY
OF HUMANITY
WAS A SABBATH, A
DAY OF REST,
A BLESSED AND
SANCTIFIED DAY.
REST IS THE
FOUNDATION OF
HUMAN LIFE,
NOT ITS
CONCLUSION.

and in our hearts: career, performance, money, status, and their counterparts must not become idols in our lives. The apostle Paul explicitly equates greed with idolatry: "Don't be greedy, for a greedy person is an idolater" (Colossians 3:5). Unless work is limited and accompanied by rest, we cannot truly experience God's design for human life.

There are people who, despite believing in God, are still anxious in their work, with excessive self-criticism, constantly telling themselves: "It's not good enough." It is evident that we should strive for excellence in our work and seek to improve, but we must not become unhealthy and obsessed. Emotionally healthy people enjoy the fruits of their labor, cultivate gratitude in their hearts, and do not constantly compare themselves to others. Therefore, protect your heart by recognizing that the ultimate giver and sustainer of your life is God. Free yourself from the need to please everyone and acknowledge that you cannot control everything. Furthermore, the frenzy of competitiveness destroys inner peace, and the inability to delegate and share tasks results in self-destructive overloads. The Sabbath principle teaches us to free ourselves from this unhealthy attachment to work and performance because our heavenly Father cares for us: "Give all your worries and cares to God, for he cares about you" (1 Peter 5:7).

Setting realistic goals in the workplace is crucial for success and well-being. While it is important to set challenging goals, it is equally important to ensure they are realistic and achievable. Avoid confusing challenges with unrealistic fantasies. The Bible warns: "A hard worker has plenty of food, but a person who chases fantasies has no sense" (Proverbs 12:11; see 28:19). Setting unrealistic goals can lead to burnout, frustration, and demoralization. Stubbornness in maintaining illusory expectations often leads to existential crises. Therefore, reexamine your expectations: Do the goals you have set for yourself depend solely and exclusively on you? Are the steps of your project practical, feasible, and attainable? To improve your goals by making them wiser, you need to simplify them. Initially, set small objectives and, as you progress in your professional development, increase the scope and reach of your goals (Matthew 25:14-30; Luke 19:11-27; 1 Timothy 3:5).

To set realistic goals you can also:

- Take stock of your abilities and better understand your strengths and weaknesses (Romans 12:3).
- Assess your actual ability to take on new commitments in the short term (Ephesians 5:16).
- Identify potential threats and obstacles (Proverbs 14:15).
- Read and analyze stories of success and failure (Proverbs 13:20).
- Obtain feedback from other people (Proverbs 24:6).
- Incorporate your goals into a broader timeline (Proverbs 14:29).

The more you study your goals and the more diligence you bring into your work, the greater your chances of success: "Good planning and hard work lead to prosperity, but hasty shortcuts lead to poverty" (Proverbs 21:5).

In the Bible, the sabbatical principle of limiting work is so serious that it also involves caring for the needy, the simplest workers, animals, and all of nature:

Plant and harvest your crops for six years, but let the land be renewed and lie uncultivated during the seventh year. Then let the poor among you harvest whatever grows on its own. Leave the rest for wild animals to eat. The same applies to your vineyards and olive groves. You have six days each week for your ordinary work, but on the seventh day you must stop working. This gives your ox and your donkey a chance to rest. It also allows your slaves and the foreigners living among you to be refreshed.

Exodus 23:10-12

These instructions call upon God's people in all times and places to raise their voices against all oppression of workers who are deprived of their rest and dignity. The apostle James explicitly warns about this issue: "For listen! Hear the cries of the field workers whom you have cheated of their pay. The cries of those who harvest your fields have reached the ears of the Lord of Heaven's Armies" (James 5:4). Limiting work, therefore, is not just an individual matter, concerning our own success and satisfaction, but is also a collective and cosmic issue, as it concerns all people and all creation.

Third, it is essential to *create cycles of rest*. The Sabbath principle is more than a formality, a mere "stopping of activities" for one day. It is a spiritual discipline that permeates our entire rhythm of life. When we study the life of Jesus, we find that throughout his ministry he maintained a Sabbath rhythm of rest, setting aside time for solitude, reflection, prayer, and contemplation:

- Jesus often withdrew to the wilderness for prayer (Luke 5:16).
- One day soon afterward Jesus went up on a mountain to pray, and he prayed to God all night (Luke 6:12).
- Before daybreak the next morning, Jesus got up and went out to an isolated place to pray (Mark 1:35).
- After telling everyone good-bye, he went up into the hills by himself to pray (Mark 6:46).

Biblically speaking, cycles of rest are primarily cycles of communion with God. As Billy Graham stated, "Nothing can calm our souls more or better prepare us for life's challenges than time spent alone with God."[6] Spending time with God is essential for our ongoing spiritual restoration. This regular time of worshiping God has both personal (Matthew 6:6) and communal (Hebrews 10:25) dimensions. All the turmoil we daily face in a world full of violence, wars, plagues, and deaths can literally drive us insane. If we learn to set aside time to cultivate our relationship with God, we will have spiritual renewal and strength to face life's storms.

Cycles of rest are also cycles of quiet. Jesus's recurring isolation from the crowds underscores the importance of making space for silence. Someone once said, "We may lack words, but may we never lack silence." Without silence, even words lose their meaning. A continuous and mixed stream of sounds makes words indistinguishable and incomprehensible. Similarly, there must be space between letters and words as graphic signs. Notice, for instance, how in this sentence you are currently reading, there is an adequate distance between each word and between each letter. This organization is what allows for the process of reading. In the same way, moments of silence and space between words are essential for mental and spiritual sanity. One minute of silence with God is worth more than weeks of inadequate speculation in your mind.

Cycles of rest also involve relationships and reflection. On the first Sabbath, the first man and woman had each other. Jesus himself regularly withdrew from the crowds with his disciples. On these occasions the Bible states that they would have time to rest and even eat properly. For example, Mark 6:31-32 says that "Jesus said to them, 'Let's go off by ourselves to a quiet place and rest awhile,' because so many people were coming and going that they didn't even have time to eat. So they went away by boat to a solitary place."

On other occasions, the Gospels reveal that during these solitary retreats, Jesus initiated deep conversations with his disciples, leading them to reflect on significant issues. We need regular time to nurture meaningful relationships and to realign our thoughts, which can get jumbled in the hustle and bustle of life. Eliminate activities from your life that no longer hold value for you. Prioritize nurturing significant relationships.

Cycles of rest are also cycles of delight and contemplation. On the first Sabbath, God rested and took pleasure in his creation. Time for contemplation is essential for souls created for beauty. The psalmist longed to contemplate the beauty of God all the days of his life (Psalm 27:4). Jesus showed how to combat anxiety through careful and reflective observation of the birds of the air and the lilies of the field (Matthew 6:25-34; Luke 12:22-34). If we do not develop a Sabbath lifestyle, we can easily be overwhelmed by the immediacy of contemporary life.

In *Receiving the Day: Christian Practices for Opening the Gift of Time*, Dorothy Bass states that "Our approach to time is so deeply ingrained in our habits that we are unaware of how powerfully it shapes us at every level. We become accustomed to a certain tempo, to unspoken rules, and soon these patterns come to feel like second nature."[7] In this context, it is worth emphasizing the importance of establishing time away from electronic devices. Cell phones give employers access to employees at any time, as well as to vendors, customers, colleagues, and competitors. Many people start and end their days with their cell phones in hand. It can also be challenging to establish cycles of rest in home office settings. Especially during the COVID-19 pandemic, home confinement and the expansion of various forms of remote work blurred the dividing line between personal life and the professional sphere. But we must not give up: it takes intelligence, determination, and conviction to prevent work from swallowing

WE MAY
LACK WORDS,
BUT MAY WE
NEVER LACK SILENCE.

up our rest times. Turn off all electronics, turn off the noise, and breathe. Develop the habit of breathing deeply. In Genesis, God breathed life into man. Breathe deeply, and with each breath, remember who is breathing life into you.

Fourth and finally, the sabbatical principle teaches us to *sleep with faith*. Rest, by definition, is restorative. It is a time to unburden oneself. Numerous scientific studies indicate that the quality and quantity of sleep are directly linked to blood pressure, blood sugar levels, immune system efficacy, memory preservation, emotional stability, and overall cognitive performance.[8] An Irish proverb says: "A good laugh and a long sleep are the best cures in the doctor's book." Indeed, there is practically no psychiatric disorder in which the person's sleep is normal. Avoiding sleep is a form of torture, not a trophy.

On the other hand, sleeping well is an indication of emotional health. In the Bible, sleep is also a spiritual theme. Sleep is a gift from a God who never sleeps and expresses our faith in his care. The psalmist states: "I lay down and slept, yet I woke up in safety, for the Lord was watching over me" (Psalm 3:5). Peaceful sleep is described as the opposite of anxiety. We can sleep because the Father does not sleep. Jesus slept peacefully in the midst of a violent storm (Mark 4:37-39). The sleep of Jesus is the sleep of peace that a fallen and restless world finds elusive.[9]

Take your nights of sleep seriously and approach the act of sleeping with faith. Develop a relaxing bedtime routine. Rest is the bridge that allows the transition from a hectic day to a peaceful night's sleep. Turn off electronic devices, lay your anxious thoughts before God, and renew your mind with the Scriptures. Be discerning, and "you can go to bed without fear; you will lie down and sleep soundly" (Proverbs 3:24).

4

Examine Your Life Regularly

What is Required in Order to Derive True Benediction
From Beholding Oneself in the Mirror of the Word?
"First of all, what is required is that thou must not look
at the mirror, not behold the mirror, but must see
thyself in the mirror."

SØREN KIERKEGAARD[1]

We deceive ourselves with remarkable frequency. In their article, "What is unrealistic optimism," Jefferson, Bortolotti, and Kuzmanovic cite three examples of self-deception that are well studied in scientific literature.

First, *the illusion of control*, where a person has an exaggerated belief that they can control independent and external events. This is commonly seen in casinos, "where people tend to think that they have a better chance at winning when they are the ones rolling the dice, and thus they bet more money in those circumstances."[2]

Second, *the better-than-average belief* (also called the superiority illusion), which is the perception of oneself, one's past behaviour, and one's lasting features as more positive than is actually the case. "An example of this better-than-average effect is when college professors are asked whether they do above-average work, and 94% of them say they do. They cannot all be right about that."[2]

Third, *unrealistic optimism,* is the "tendency for people to believe that they are less likely to experience negative events and more likely to experience positive events than are other people. An example of the optimism bias is when people underestimate the likelihood that their marriage will end in divorce or that they will develop a serious health condition during their lives."[2] There are people who simply do not adequately reflect on their own lives. A life without self-examination inevitably leads to frustration, disappointment, and all kinds of unnecessary suffering.

Self-examination is a central discipline in the Christian spiritual tradition. It involves deep reflection on life in the light of the Word of God with the help of God himself. The Bible warns: "People may be right in their own eyes, but the Lord examines their heart" (Proverbs 21:2). It is much easier for a person to assume they are right and others are wrong than to sincerely examine their own life. We can deceive others and even ourselves, but we cannot deceive God (Galatians 6:7-8). The wisdom of self-examination lies in honestly evaluating our lives so that we can be what God wants us to be and not what our flesh has accepted as permissible. Through self-examination in the fear of the Lord, we dispel illusions in our understanding of ourselves, increase our trust in God, prove the health of our spiritual life, and become better equipped to help others.

Unfortunately, many people are good at examining the lives of others but incapable of examining their own. Jesus warned against the hypocrisy of pointing out the speck in others' eyes without first removing the huge log from one's own eyes (Matthew 7:3). Although it is much easier to see the sins and faults of others, Paul exhorted the church in Corinth: "Examine yourselves to see if your faith is genuine. Test yourselves. Surely you know that Jesus Christ is among you; if not, you have failed the test of genuine faith" (2 Corinthians13:5). The Greek word translated as "examine" in this text is *peirazo*, which refers to a test, a trial, an intense inspection with the purpose of proving something. Self-examination is not a trivial, routine procedure done hastily and superficially. For example, many Christians have the habit of starting their prayers by asking God for forgiveness in repentance for any sins they may have committed. While this habit is important, it does not exactly constitute self-examination. As we learn from the Scriptures, self-examination is a much more comprehensive and profound process than simply a prayer for purification; it involves reflection, confrontation, and character development.

The Scriptures teach that self-examination is not merely self-criticism. Notice that Paul stated that the Corinthians surely "know that Jesus Christ is among you" (2 Corinthians 13:5). The presence of the Lord himself is what distinguishes Christian self-examination. God's servants do not examine themselves based on their own understanding, for "the human heart is the most deceitful of all things, and desperately wicked. Who really knows how bad it is?" (Jeremiah 17:9). If we rely solely on ourselves, we can easily fall into extremes. Some consider themselves pure, filled with self-justification, while others become depressed, filled with self-pity. In both cases, the criteria for evaluation are wrong and there is a considerable dose of pride.

Therefore, in Christian self-examination, the criterion for analysis is the gospel of Jesus. Christ's work on the cross reveals, on the one hand, the violence and malevolence of our sin, and on the other, the grandeur and power of God's love. In Christ's death and resurrection, we understand our own identity, the seriousness of our sin, and the blessing of the new life we receive in him. We are not transformed by being absorbed in ourselves, but by contemplating the glory of Christ (2 Corinthians 3:18). Scottish minister Robert Murray M'Cheyne counseled: "for every look at yourself, take ten looks at Christ."[3]

We live in an era where our lives are monitored through various technological gadgets. Harvard professor Shoshana Zuboff states that "there was a time when you searched Google, but now Google searches you."[4] Some people obsessively monitor and evaluate their own daily physical performance: number of

FOR THOSE
WHO CONSIDER
THEMSELVES PURE,
THE CROSS IS NOT
NECESSARY;
FOR THOSE
WHO CONSIDER
THEMSELVES
WORTHLESS,
THE CROSS IS NOT
SUFFICIENT.

steps, heart rate, blood pressure, etc. Researcher Deborah Lupton asserts that we live in the age of the quantified self, quantified human beings.[5] Yet God knows us better than any device that exists or will ever exist. He knows the depths of our spirit. He knows us better than we know ourselves. The Lord is entirely trustworthy, and he establishes the parameters for evaluation in his Word. Thus, in Christian self-examination, we cry out for the help of God Himself, just as the psalmist did: "Search me, O God, and know my heart; test me and know my anxious thoughts. Point out anything in me that offends you, and lead me along the path of everlasting life" (Psalm 139:23-24).

When people look in the mirror, they see a reflection of themselves. People need to look into the spiritual mirror and examine their spiritual reality, measuring their lives by the standard of the Word of God (James 1:22-25). Bible verse tattoos don't protect us. T-shirts, stickers, and bracelets with evangelical phrases are not capable of changing our lives. The Word needs to transform us from the inside out. Therefore, read and reflect on essential biblical texts about Christian conduct, such as the Beatitudes (Matthew 5:1-12), the works of the flesh and the fruit of the Spirit (Galatians 5:19-23), and the Ten Commandments (Exodus 20:1-21). Honestly ask yourself if you see any of these attitudes or behaviors in your life. But always conduct this examination in the fear of the Lord and in His presence. God is the one who humbles us to recognize our mistakes, and it is he who refreshes us and fills us with hope. God Himself examines and tests us: "But I, the Lord, search all hearts and examine secret motives. I give all people their due rewards, according to what their actions deserve" (Jeremiah 17:10).

Self-examination should be conducted regularly. The fact that someone has served the Lord for years does not mean they are living in a way that pleases God today (1 Corinthians 10:12).

THE FACT THAT
SOMEONE HAS
SERVED
THE LORD FOR YEARS
DOES NOT MEAN
THAT THEY ARE
CURRENTLY
LIVING IN A WAY
THAT IS PLEASING
TO GOD.

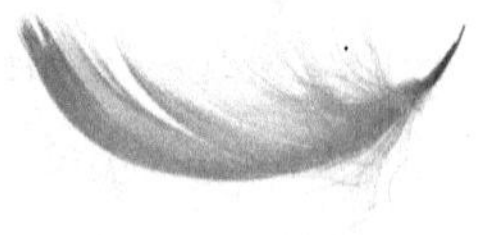

Thus, we are called to perform self-examination with God during the solemn act of the Lord's Supper: "That is why you should examine yourself before eating the bread and drinking the cup" (1 Corinthians 11:28). No area of life should be spared. Be wary of yourself. It is necessary to examine motivations, words, thoughts, actions, reactions, insecurities, perplexities, relationships, studies, work, finances, pains, pleasures, in short, all of life. We need to reflect and pray as Job did: "Tell me, what have I done wrong? Show me my rebellion and my sin" (Job 13:23). Once we identify sin in our lives, we need to confess and renounce it. We often have difficulty admitting errors, but we need to be humble and recognize them. Do not seek self-justification. To justify a mistake is to make another mistake. The Bible teaches that God forgives confessed sins, not flimsy excuses (1 John 1:5-10; Proverbs 28:13). When a believer is honest and open before God, there will be continuous spiritual growth.

Many people practice the *nightly examination of conscience,* carried out before going to sleep. The psalmist stated: "I think of the good old days, long since ended, when my nights were filled with joyful songs. I search my soul and ponder the difference now" (Psalm 77:5-6). In this nightly self-examination, we can reflect on our day and, above all, the state of our conscience. Is it good (1 Timothy 1:5, NIV), and clear (1 Timothy 3:9), and pure (Hebrews 9:14)? Or is it weak (1 Corinthians 8:7), corrupted (Titus 1:15), and dead (1 Timothy 4:2)? Being human, we are all prone to errors and imbalance if we do not dedicate time to self-examination and life review. Once we develop this daily habit, we will have a greater capacity to live with a conscience free of offenses against God and people (Acts 24:16).

Historically, *fasting and prayer* are also habits associated with self-examination. The Scriptures indicate that through fasting and praying, we can enhance our sense of humility and remind ourselves of how much we need God, providing the proper mindset for self-examination. An additional practice in this process is *keeping a spiritual journal*. Having a notebook to regularly write down your prayers, anxieties, joys, and biblical reflections is a strategy widely practiced by Christians around the world. Writing allows us to record our thoughts and examine them. For example, the book of Esther recounts that on one occasion the king, unable to sleep, began to reflect on the book of chronicles of his reign (Esther 6:1). In addition to reflection, keeping a journal allows us to better observe what triggers good or bad feelings in our lives. This is a good practice for becoming more spiritually and emotionally aware.

Christian self-examination involves a serious reflection of our emotions and feelings. Emotions occupy a central place in our journey. The complexity of emotions corresponds to the complexity of human life itself. Don't be superficial when dealing with your temperament. It is beneficial to describe and name more precisely what you are feeling. When someone asks, "How are you?," we regularly respond, "I'm fine." But "fine" is not a feeling; it is just a standard, polite response. The problem arises when we are evasive and imprecise with ourselves. Thus, at the right time, reflect in detail on what really makes you "fine." Be more specific: "I feel grateful," "enthusiastic," "peaceful."

The University of Berkeley released a study that identified 27 basic human emotions: "admiration, adoration, aesthetic appreciation, amusement, anger, anxiety, awe, awkwardness, boredom, calmness, confusion, craving, disgust, empathic pain, entrancement, excitement, fear, horror, interest, joy, nostalgia, relief, romance, sadness, satisfaction, sexual desire, surprise."[6] Naming these feelings is an excellent exercise in truly understanding that, as the poet Fernando Pessoa wrote, we can give "to each emotion a personality, to each state of mind a soul."[7]

From time to time, it is valuable to hold *spiritual retreats* for calm and deep reflection. We saw in the previous chapter that the Lord Jesus himself regularly held prayer and reflection retreats. We can take advantage of seasonal changes, holidays, vacations, New Year's Eve, the end of the semester, and other opportunities for self-examination. Take inventory of your own life. Review and reflect on your calendar, your email, and your responsibilities. Set aside time to reflect, for example:

- How many new friends have I made?
- Which edifying books have I read?
- Whom have I made happy?
- What is the ratio of good words to bad words that have come out of my mouth?
- Which talents have I developed?
- What are my motivations?
- How am I reacting to the disappointments of life?
- Am I truly a witness of the gospel?

Spiritual ostentation does not save anyone (Luke 16:15; 2 Corinthians 10:18). Jesus spoke extensively about the self-righteousness of hypocritical religious leaders (Matthew 23:23-29). They said the right words and wore the right clothes, but inwardly they lived in spiritual filth. They were wolves in sheep's clothing. Those who take the spiritual discipline of self-examination seriously also take seriously Jesus's warning that not everyone who calls on his name will enter the kingdom of heaven (Matthew 7:21-23). Therefore, "let us test and examine our ways. Let us turn back to the LORD" (Lamentations 3:40).

5
Take Care of Your Body

I am a heart beating in the world.

CLARICE LISPECTOR [1]

The integration between physical, mental, and spiritual health is evident in the Scriptures. Proverbs states that those who embrace wisdom receive life and "healing to their whole body" (Proverbs 4:22). Similarly, "a cheerful heart is good medicine" (Proverbs 17:22). The apostle John, in greeting his friend, says: "Dear friend, I hope all is well with you and that you are as healthy in body as you are strong in spirit" (3 John 1:2). Paul also prayed for the Thessalonians's health in all its dimensions: "Now may the God of peace make you holy in every way, and may your whole spirit and soul and body be kept blameless until our Lord Jesus Christ comes again" (1 Thessalonians 5:23). The Bible teaches that taking care of one's own body is a fundamental human duty: "No one hates his own body but feeds and cares for it, just as Christ cares for the church" (Ephesians 5:29). For Christians, the body is a temple of God, inhabited by the Holy Spirit (1 Corinthians 6:19-20). Therefore, the body should not be idolized (as it is not God), but neither should it be despised and treated with disdain (as it is a temple). Promoting physical well-being is a way to honor God. In this chapter, we will specifically highlight three aspects of bodily care: we must *nourish* the body, *exercise* the body, and *care* for the body.

First of all, we need to *properly nourish our bodies.*

THE BIBLE BEGINS AND ENDS WITH MEALS. GOD'S FIRST WORDS TO HUMANITY ARE AN INVITATION TO EAT; THE FINAL VISION OF THE WORLD IS A FESTIVE WEDDING BANQUET.

"Whenever people come to the table, they demonstrate with the unmistakable evidence of their stomachs that they are not self-subsisting gods. They are finite and mortal creatures dependent on God's many good gifts: sunlight, photosynthesis, decomposition, soil fertility, water, bees and butterflies, chickens, sheep, cows, gardeners, farmers, cooks, strangers and friends (the list goes on and on). Eating reminds us that we partake in a grace-world, a blessed creation worthy of attention, care and celebration."[2]

It is interesting to note that the Bible begins and ends with meals. God's first words to humanity are an invitation to eat; the first conflict in the Bible arises because of a forbidden meal; Jesus's first miracle involved turning water into wine; Jesus's last act before his death was sharing a supper with bread and wine; and the final vision of the world is a festive wedding banquet. Food is a central theological theme.[3]

Over the centuries, Christian theologians have reflected on the superabundance of God, who lives eternally in a mutual sharing of nourishing love, truth, goodness, and beauty among the Father, Son, and Holy Spirit. God's gift was graciously shared with creation and humanity. Creation is a cosmic banquet and an interdependent network of edible signs that participates in the divine sharing. Human sin disrupted the nourishing community of creation. In response, the Incarnation is the radical sharing of God, who became the very food at the Eucharistic banquet. Jesus Christ, the Living Bread who came down from heaven, reoriented the interdependence between human communities, between humanity and creation, and between all creation and God.

In the Christian perspective, it is not only what we eat that matters, but also how we eat. "So whether you eat or drink or whatever you do, do it all for the glory of God" (1 Corinthians 10:31).[4] When faced with any meal, we need to be aware that

God is the Lord of life. Neither food nor diet should be idols in our hearts. The desire for food must not dominate your life. Paul spoke about people whose god is their stomach (Philippians 3:19) and warned against uncontrolled and harmful desires (2 Timothy 1:7; see Proverbs 23:20-21). Many people develop compulsive eating habits. In difficult situations such as frustration, stress, loneliness, and sadness, they begin to overeat in search of comfort, consolation, and escape. Jesus taught that life is more than food (Luke 12:23) and that "People do not live by bread alone, but by every word that comes from the mouth of God" (Matthew 4:4). Self-control is a fruit of the Holy Spirit in the lives of Jesus's disciples. Therefore, to properly nourish our bodies, we should avoid the excess of foods notoriously harmful to human health, such as processed foods, fats, sugars, and so on.

In her book, *Less of Me: A 30-Day Devotional for Your Weight Loss Journey*, Becky Lehman states that Christians need to be more mindful when they are eating. Indeed, through prayer before meals, it is possible to give thanks for the gift of food, intercede for those who need provision, and ask for self-control from the Spirit of God.[5]

In our nutrition, we must also avoid the other extreme, namely, the idolatry of diet, the deification of the body and appearance. Some people have begun to exalt rigid diets and ascetic practices as a form of salvation, an attitude expressly condemned in the Scriptures (Colossians 2:16-23). In fact, ceremonial dietary rules were of great importance to early Christian communities, as they historically were some of the defining marks of the Israelites. Levitical law classified foods as clean and unclean, that is, suitable and unsuitable for human consumption, and outlined ceremonial procedures for the preparation and enjoyment of meals. But from Christ on, all foods were considered pure (Mark 7:14-23; Acts 10:9-28; 1 Corinthians 8:1-13; 10:23-33; 1 Timothy

4:3-5). The Lord Jesus himself was not an ascetic and regularly and joyfully participated in meals. This behavior led his enemies to accuse him of being a "glutton and a drunkard" (Matthew 11:19; Luke 7:34). The obviously false accusation came from hypocritical religious leaders who could not tolerate Jesus's sociable and joyful approach, which valued the beauty of life created by God. Jesus taught and demonstrated that eating is a legitimate time for joy, satisfaction, and gratitude for the sons and daughters of God.

Thus, as we nourish our bodies, we should learn to savor our food. As Ecclesiastes states: "So go ahead. Eat your food with joy, and drink your wine with a happy heart, for God approves of this!" (Ecclesiastes 9:7).

There are two biblical proverbs that wisely guide the habit of eating: "My child, eat honey, for it is good, and the honeycomb is sweet to the taste" (Proverbs 24:13); and "Do you like honey? Don't eat too much, or it will make you sick!" (Proverbs 25:16). A well-nourished person knows how to both enjoy and limit their food intake. In the Portuguese language, the connection between the terms "saber" (to know) and "sabor" (flavor) is very interesting. Both terms have roots in the Latin word *sapio* or *sapere*, which means both "to understand," "to know," and "to have taste," "to have flavor." The connection between wisdom and eating is unquestionable.

Often when people enter into deep depression, they lose their appetite and start to waste away. The biblical episode of Elijah in the cave is instructive in this regard. In the prophet's time of deep discouragement, the Lord God himself led him to a period of rest and nourishment. While Elijah was sleeping, an angel touched him and said: "Get up and eat!" (1 Kings 19:5). Elijah then ate, drank, and lay down again. After repeating this process, the Bible reports that "he got up and ate and drank, and the food gave him enough strength to travel forty days and forty nights to Mount Sinai, the mountain of God" (1 Kings 19:8). Another emblematic episode is recorded in Acts: a ship with 276 people on board faced a storm and was adrift. Paul then insisted that everyone eat. "'You have been so worried that you haven't touched food for two weeks,' he said. 'Please eat something now for your own good'" (Acts 27:33-34). After taking the bread and giving thanks to God in the presence of everyone, Paul broke it into pieces and ate it. "Then everyone was encouraged and began to eat" (Acts 27:36).

The gospel teaches us the importance of nutrition not only for ourselves but for all people. May we also extend our hand to those in need who need bread. In *The Theology of Food: Eating and the Eucharist*, Angel F. Mendez Montoya reminds us that the Eucharist is the greatest paradigm of culinary epistemology and ontology.[6] Jesus himself is the ultimate nourishment that sustains and satisfies our lives. It is wise to rethink our eating habits: we can undergo a dietary detox, reevaluate the amount of food we put on our plates, avoid fatty foods, increase consumption of fruits, vegetables, legumes, and whole grains, be more grateful for the food we have, serve hungry people with more love and mercy, and better appreciate meal times by understanding their spiritual significance through the gospel.

Secondly, we should *exercise our bodies*. According to the World Health Organization, worldwide prevalence of obesity more than doubled between 1990 and 2022.[7] Among the main factors cited are not only the consumption of high-fat and sugary foods but also drastic changes in people's lifestyles. People have become more physically inactive. The sedentary nature of new forms of work, urbanization, and new modes of transportation have been identified as inhibiting factors for physical activity. Today's workers spend long periods sitting, significantly increasing their risk of diseases. The Sanford Health System has asserted that prolonged sitting is "the new smoking" and a true "silent killer."[8]

In this context, we must keep in mind that the Bible substantially affirms movement as an important characteristic of the human body. By synthesizing human life in God, Paul stated that: "For in him we live and *move* and exist" (Acts 17:28). Movement is life: our hearts beat, our lungs inhale and exhale, our blood circulates throughout our bodies. Exercising, therefore, promotes our physical and mental well-being in several ways: increasing vitality; strengthening muscles; reducing blood pressure; providing pleasant emotions with the release of endorphins; regulating blood sugar; improving heart function; reducing stress, anxiety, and depression; and increasing sleep quality at night.

Paul, in particular, used multiple athletic metaphors and terminology in his writings.[9] He feared that all his missionary activity had been in vain (Galatians 2:2; Philippians 2:16), and rebuked the Galatian Christians: "You were running the race so well. Who has held you back from following the truth?" (Galatians 5:7). In Romans 9:16, he states that mercy depends only on God, and not on our running, that is, on our own efforts. In Philippians 1:27-30, he encourages the church to act as a tactically adjusted team. In Colossians, he states that he struggles for the believers (Colossians 1:29-2:1), just like Epaphras (Colossians 4:12). Paul's desire was to run towards the finish line and receive the heavenly prize (Philippians 3:12-14). At the end of his life, he stated that he had completed the race (2 Timothy 4:7-8). There are many other references to athletic practices in Paul's writings,[10] but I will highlight three passages:

> Don't you realize that in a race everyone runs, but only one person gets the prize? So run to win! All athletes are disciplined in their

training. They do it to win a prize that will fade away, but we do it
for an eternal prize. So I run with purpose in every step. I am not
just shadowboxing. I discipline my body like an athlete, training it
to do what it should. Otherwise, I fear that after preaching to others
I myself might be disqualified.

1 Corinthians 9:24-27

Physical training is good, but training for godliness is much better,
promising benefits in this life and in the life to come.

1 Timothy 4:8

And athletes cannot win the prize unless they follow the rules.

2 Timothy 2:5

In the combined reading of these texts, we learn that Paul
considered physical exercise a legitimate and valuable activity,
capable of promoting not only a healthy physical and mental condition but also character. Paul associates sports practice with the
development of discipline, patience, steadfastness of purpose,
overcoming challenges, creativity, and responsibility. In light of
these biblical teachings, consider reflecting on your life and improving your athletic habits. Take responsibility for your health
(Galatians 6:5) and avoid making excuses (Ecclesiastes 11:4).

We often associate exercise with something that has to be puni-
tive and unpleasant, which is why we avoid or procrastinate until we can do something "official," like going to a well-equipped
gym. But exercising the body doesn't require expensive equip-
ment or traveling across the city to a gym. While it is certainly
beneficial to be at the gym, it's also possible to stretch, work
in a garden, or sweep leaves. Walking is one of the universally
known ways to stay fit and healthy, and it is a free and effective
activity. It is encouraging to know that we have many options

and interesting ways to move our bodies and exercise. It doesn't matter how we choose to move, as long as we do it. Find someone to exercise with you. A companion can encourage perseverance in the routine (Ecclesiastes 4:9-10). And remember that the Lord Himself is always by your side (Matthew 28:20).

Thirdly, it is necessary to *take care of your body*. It is not wise to poison the body with vices, nor to ignore the resources of medicine. Often, we are struck by physical illnesses and insist on continuing our activities. In the face of illnesses, we can pray with faith (James 5:14-15), for God is powerful to heal and restore human health (Psalm 41:3). But as emphasized in the introduction of this book, praying for healing does not negate the importance of seeking help from doctors and healthcare professionals if necessary. The Christian church itself decisively aided the development of modern medicine by creating hospital institutions and medical schools and establishing values and practices aimed at the care of integral human health.

Therefore, it is wise to have regular medical check-ups. Just as God, in His mercy, provides us with resources to use wisely, time to manage well, relationships to develop with love, and talents to multiply, he also gives us a body to manage well. Regular medical exams can help reveal potential health problems before they worsen. Early detection gives us the opportunity to obtain treatment and avoid complications, increasing the chances of a cure. By closely monitoring our physical condition, we reduce unnecessary health costs and suffering and increase our quality and life expectancy. Often, a person may speculate about a thousand things concerning their health, feeling sad and disheartened. A simple check-up can reveal some easily remedied nutritional deficit.

Unfortunately, many people live in extremely precarious conditions, without basic sanitation, adequate food, medicine, and medical treatment. This fact should be a decisive stimulus for Christians around the world who have the means to properly care for their own bodies to be attentive, mobilized, and pre-pared to assist those in need. When we take care of our bodies, we can indeed be "always ready to do what is good" (Titus 3:1). Jesus "gave his life to free us from every kind of sin, to cleanse us, and to make us his very own people, totally committed to doing good deeds" (Titus 2:14). There is no doubt that a life dedicated to serving others will be more fruitful with a healthy body. We use our arms to lift the fallen, our hands to carry supplies, our legs to travel to places where people need help. It is a privilege for Christians to seek the purification from anything that contam-inates the body or spirit (2 Corinthians 7:1). May we indeed offer our bodies to God as a living and holy sacrifice (Romans 12:1).

6
Maintain Mental Hygiene

Thinking drives you crazy. Think about it.

ANONYMOUS

Maintaining mental hygiene is fundamental for both sanity and sanctity. In Philippians 4:8, we are instructed to focus on "what is true, and honorable, and right, and pure, and lovely, and admirable" and to "think about things that are excellent and worthy of praise." This biblical text implies that we have the power to govern our thoughts and, therefore, we are responsible for them. In other words, we can and should exercise strict control over this area of our lives, which many never think about controlling.

Our mind is not a garbage can. Think twice before harboring trash and refuse inside your head. We have the ability to decide what we will allow to remain in our thoughts and what we should leave outside. A person who does not master their own spirit is compared to a destroyed city, without walls, where anyone can enter and anyone can leave (Proverbs 25:28). If our thoughts are orderly, our external life will be as well. Thoughts shape our actions. Sooner or later, what has been a stream of thoughts in a person's life will appear and manifest itself, becoming visible in their actions. Just as a flash of lightning foreshadows the roar of thunder, the thoughts we cultivate often foreshadow our actions in the external world.

It is no coincidence that the Apostle Paul continues his argument to the Philippians by saying: "Keep putting into practice all you learned" (Philippians 4:9). Practice follows thoughts.

When we walk along a major avenue, such as Avenida Paulista in São Paulo, we are impressed by the grandeur and stability of the buildings. It is interesting to consider that all those buildings began as mere thoughts and ideas.

In this chapter, therefore, *we will think about how we think.* We will specifically highlight the following attitudes taught in the Scriptures: eliminating depressing thoughts, cultivating virtuous thoughts, and reeducating the memory.

Thinking is like tidying up a house. First, we must *eliminate repetitive negative thoughts.* Just like dust, sad thoughts come from all directions: professional frustrations, gratuitous offenses, financial losses, injustices, hopelessness over the behavior of someone we love, resentments of all kinds, ministerial discouragement, the loss of a loved one, and dissatisfaction with one's professional performance.

The disappointments of life are common. What is uncommon is feeding bitter thoughts. This habit, also known as depressive rumination, causes all kinds of problems for mental health. A person keeps thinking and rethinking cyclically about things that went wrong, which makes it difficult to relax and switch off the mind. Their thoughts are only focused on failures and mistakes, and not on ways to improve things. Negative rumination projects problems into the future, painting a distorted horizon. Excessive thoughts overload the mind, making even simple everyday decisions difficult, like choosing clothes to wear. The person loses the ability to accomplish simple tasks because they become lost within themselves. The anguished psalmist said: "My heart is sick, withered like grass, and I have lost my appetite" (Psalm 102:4).

We must be careful. When you cling to sad thoughts, you can draw the worst possible conclusions from your emotions, not from the facts.

Heavy thoughts have the power to bring us down. Notice that it is precisely the notion of weight that shapes the term "depression," which comes from the Latin *deprimire,* meaning "to press down, to depress." The literal meaning of the term depression is closely linked to the psychological meaning of the term that became popular in the 19th century,[1] that is, a feeling of internal weight, a state of sadness, a crushing of the spirit. In fact, exhaustion and sadness impact our expression and posture. We don't have the energy to stand up, our eyelids feel heavy, our shoulders slump, our heads tilt, and our backs hunch.

Moments of sadness are inevitable along our journey on this earth. As we read in chapter 1, there is a time to mourn and weep. But it is quite different to cultivate bitterness in our soul. The Scriptures explicitly condemn this behavior: "Look after each other so that none of you fails to receive the grace of God. Watch out that no poisonous root of bitterness grows up to trouble you, corrupting many" (Hebrews 12:15). Evil thoughts want to take root in our spirit like a poisonous plant. They grow and affect not only the person but also those around them. Therefore, do not water bitter thoughts. It is foolish to take seriously what we should turn our backs on. Many genuinely important things lose their value in our hearts when we disregard them, while others of no importance grow because we give them too much attention. Thus, we are instructed: "Get rid of all bitterness, rage, anger, harsh words, and slander, as well as all types of evil behavior" (Ephesians 4:31).

How should we eliminate bitter thoughts? The first step is to identify the source of these negative thoughts. In Proverbs 14:10 it says: "Each heart knows its own bitterness." Hence the importance of developing the habit of self-examination, as we saw in chapter four. Ask God for help in identifying the sources of your frustrations and negative thoughts. How did they start? What

AS A FLASH OF LIGHTING FORESHADOWS THE ROAR OF THUNDER, THE THOUGHTS WE CULTIVATE OFTEN FORESHADOW OUR ACTIONS IN THE EXTERNAL WORLD.

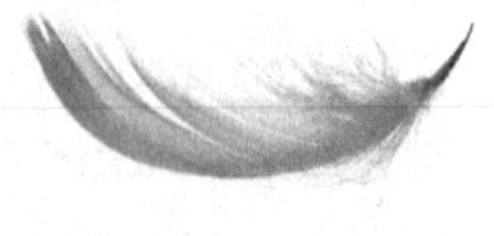

triggered them? What was the circumstance? If necessary, write down your concerns. I know a man who has an interesting habit. When wakes up worried at night, he simply takes paper and pen and writes down his worries. Then he prays, handing the situation over to God, places the paper on his bedside table, and sleeps peacefully. This man said, "When I transcribe the problem to paper, I feel the worry leaving my mind. There is nothing I can do to solve it before I go to sleep. So I set it aside and sleep. The next day, at the right time, I will face that problem again." Jesus himself taught his disciples to limit their worries: "Today's trouble is enough for today" (Matthew 6:34).

When bitter thoughts overwhelm you, cut them off abruptly. Don't fall into the trap of reprocessing them. Don't allow yourself to be alone with them. Read a book, take a walk, call a friend, watch a movie, visit someone. If you work indoors and suffer from negative thoughts, try to let in as much natural light as possible. Open windows and curtains, try to bring the outside world in. Don't live walled in. Cultivate plants near you. Enjoy the sunset. Walk outdoors and engage in activities that involve multiple senses. Eliminate addictions from your life: substances such as drugs and alcohol can contribute to perpetuating feelings of sadness. Develop new skills. Do something completely new, something you have literally never done before, like practicing a different sport, learning culinary techniques, traveling and exploring new destinations, or simply walking in a part of your own neighborhood that you have never explored before.

The lack of new stimuli — seeing the same walls, the same people, the same news over and over again — can be a breeding ground for repetitive thoughts, especially if you are already prone to them. When you do exactly the same things day after day, you use the same parts of your brain. Engaging in new activities can bring the emotional pleasure of reward and improve your mental state and well-being.

Secondly, *cultivate virtuous thoughts*. As John Stott said: "If we want to live rightly, we must think rightly."[2] It is necessary to reclaim our mental territory. In the face of the overwhelming challenges of daily life, the mind needs space to reorder itself, and this does not happen spontaneously. It is not enough to vegetate in front of a television and expect thoughts to become reordered and virtuous. A conscious effort is needed to fill the mental space with restorative thoughts.

This mental reconfiguration is also spiritual, as stated in Romans 8:6: "So letting your sinful nature control your mind leads to death. But letting the Spirit control your mind leads to life and peace." Without a transformation of the mind, thoughts will be drawn to what is worthless, just as flies are attracted to a piece of rotten meat. Based on this biblical principle, Dr. Saundra Dalton-Smith discusses the importance of creating a "mental sanctuary," that is, a sacred place for the mind to rest. Dalton-Smith suggests, for example, that one way to create a mental sanctuary is to choose a characteristic of God and reflect on it throughout the day: "Let each characteristic be the mental place you return to throughout the day as you practice creating a mental sanctuary."[3] One can reflect on God's love, joy, peace, kindness, goodness, gentleness, faithfulness, and mercy, and so on. King David had this habit: "I lie awake thinking of you, meditating on you through the night" (Psalm 63:6).

As we have seen, the apostle Paul insisted on this point in Philippians 4:8, indicating what the fabric of our thoughts should be:

- We must think about everything that is *true*, and not about pernicious lies and sophistries. The human heart is the most deceitful of all things (Jeremiah 17:9), and the devil is the father of lies (John 8:44). When something goes wrong, we are tempted to think the worst, but we should focus on what is true. Ask yourself: Is this thought true? Is it aligned with the Word of God?

- We must think about everything that is *noble,* and not about what is dishonorable and foolish. Many people become emotionally ill because they fill their minds with gossip, nonsense, and slander against others. Ask yourself: Is this thought honest? Is its intention genuine and honorable?

- We must think about everything that is *right,* and not about injustices. We can ask ourselves: Is this thought right in light of the Word of God? Is it just and innocent?

- We must think about everything that is *pure,* and not about what is contaminated and morally dirty. Keep the Word of God in your heart and use it as protection against impure thoughts (Psalm 119:11). Ask yourself: Is this thought pure and clean?

- We must think about everything that is *lovely and admirable,* and not about what is despicable and repugnant. Many people would not want their thoughts to be exposed on a public screen. However, God is constantly aware of what we are thinking. Ask yourself: Is this thought pleasing to God?

- We must think about everything that is *excellent and praiseworthy.* Ask yourself: Is there any virtue in this thought? Does it lead us to praise God?

Third, to maintain the hygiene of the mind, it is necessary to *educate the memory.* Unfortunately, the human memory is deceitful. It fails us when we most need it and works when it shouldn't. In her work *The Future of Nostalgia,* cultural theorist Svetlava Boym states that "nostalgia is not always about the past; it can

WITHOUT A TRANSFORMATION OF THE MIND, THOUGHTS WILL BE DRAWN TO WHAT IS WORTHLESS, JUST AS FLIES ARE ATTRACTED TO A PIECE OF ROTTEN MEAT.

be both retrospective (looking backwards) but also prospective (looking forwards). Often, fantasies of the past determined by needs of the present needs have a direct impact on realities of the future."[4] In any case, there is a distortion of reality in the person's mind. It is important to educate the memory, as it can either determine heaven or hell. Paul explicitly said, "[B]ut I focus on this one thing: Forgetting the past and looking forward to what lies ahead, I press on to reach the end of the race and receive the heavenly prize for which God, through Christ Jesus, is calling us" (Philippians 3:13-14). We should not rummage through the garbage of the past. No one makes spiritual progress by looking back. On the road of life, the past is a dead end. That's why Paul emphasizes moving forward, toward the goal: Christ.

The Bible teaches that the past should be a source of wisdom, not torment. We should recall only what brings hope (Lamentations 3:21). I remember an occasion when I was eight years old and felt very sad. I don't remember the reason for my sadness, but I recall my mother's words to console me. She said, "Son, don't be sad. I love you very much. The day you were born, I was so happy!" She said this with such strength and sincerity that my sadness instantly disappeared. Knowing that my mother was so happy when I was born was comforting to me. To this day, I hold onto that thought. It's one of the joys I recall to bring hope to my heart.

Thus, replay those happy experiences, the pleasant memories. Life regularly gives us lessons. We need to pay attention to what God wants to teach us. You cannot change the past, but God can change how the past affects you.

7

Celebrate, Pray, and Give Thanks

Celebrations bring balance to life. Life itself is serious
and demanding. Celebrations lighten the mood,
making us more relaxed and authentic.

LUIZ MIGUEL DUARTE[1]

n one of the most psychologically powerful passages of the Bible, Paul affirms to the Thessalonian Christians: "Always be joyful. Never stop praying. Be thankful in all circumstances, for this is God's will for you who belong to Christ Jesus" (1 Thessalonians 5:16-18). The verses mention three attitudes in the Christian life that permeate everything: rejoicing, praying, and giving thanks.

Paul's text is assertive. We are to practice these actions continuously, without ceasing. Not only in pleasant moments, but in all moments. And it's not about praying or expressing gratitude as mere formal acts, but about developing a grateful and confident spirit in God. It's also not about stoic resignation. It is about Christian praise. In other words, we cannot control all circumstances, but we can respond to them by exercising faith in God and recognizing His sovereignty in every detail of our lives. We can be thankful in all circumstances because everything works together for the good of those who love God. No matter the tribulation, it is invariably accompanied by divine mercy. Circumstances change, but God does not.

First, we need to *rejoice*. To live with emotional and spiritual integrity, we must learn to value moments of joy. Presbyterian pastor Elben César stated, "Joy is not just a life option. It is a command of God to his people."[2] The Bible teaches that there is a time to weep, but also a time to laugh, celebrate, and rejoice. In her

A CHRISTIAN DOES NOT SIMPLY SAY "AMEN" TO LIFE'S SITUATIONS, BUT "HALLELUJAH" TO GOD DESPITE THE CIRCUMSTANCES.

article, "The Powerful Authority of Cute Animals," theologian and writer Beatrice Marovich examines the fascination that animals hold over people. Often, when a pet does something "cute," humans stop what they're doing just to watch, appreciate, and laugh.[3] Indeed, tenderness is not a luxury but a human necessity.

Jesus taught his disciples to live with an unguarded spirit, to move through life contentedly, without being a burden to anyone. There is an evident spiritual dimension in Christian joy, as it is a joy given by the Lord Jesus Himself through His Word: "I have told you these things so that you will be filled with my joy. Yes, your joy will overflow!" (John 15:11). This joy that comes from Christ Himself is superlative, referred to as a "glorious, inexpressible joy" (1 Peter 1:8) that develops in us through the action of the Holy Spirit (Galatians 5:22).

Therefore, take joy seriously. Surround yourself with happy people. Joy generates more joy. The wisdom of Proverbs teaches: "Don't befriend angry people or associate with hot-tempered people, or you will learn to be like them and endanger your soul" (Proverbs 22:24-25). Laugh at yourself and don't take yourself too seriously. Knowing how to laugh at yourself is essential for freeing oneself from inappropriate lifestyles. The writer Amos Oz, in his famous essay "How to Cure a Fanatic," asserts that the ability to live with a greater sense of humor is a hallmark of people who promote peace. On the other hand, fanatics are incapable of laughing at themselves. In Oz's words: "Humor is the ability to see yourself as others may see you, humor is the capacity to realize that no matter how righteous you are and how terribly wronged you have been, there is a certain side to life that is always a bit funny."[4]

A sense of humor helps individuals understand their own limits and be less critical of themselves, opening doors to a lighter and more intelligent life. For example, in a society of exhibitionists, writer Camila Fremder, who considers herself an antisocial homebody, developed a humorous way to connect with other antisocial people. She created the Association of the Charisma-Less, a virtual community that surpassed 20,000 people in its first years. There is no doubt that good humor is powerful for mental health and relationships.

Celebrating life is a blessing. For those who fear God, life is a gift, a present. After all, "whatever is good and perfect is a gift coming down to us from God our Father who created all the lights in the heavens" (James 1:17). Everything good we receive comes from God. Life may be precarious, but it is precious. "Therefore," says the author of Ecclesiastes, "Eat your food with joy, and drink your wine with a happy heart, for God approves of this! Wear fine clothes, with a splash of cologne! Live happily with the woman you love through all the meaningless days of life that God has given you under the sun" (Ecclesiastes 9:7-9). The Bible speaks of the legitimate pleasure of being alive. In this passage, especially, we see touch, smell, taste, sight, and hearing mobilized in enjoying the God-given life. The text says that "God approves of this," proclaiming liberation to the unhappy. The immediate context is very interesting, for Ecclesiastes addresses the perplexities of life. In other words, the struggles of life cannot desensitize us to the point of losing our joy.

In the New Testament, Paul wrote that he "learned how to be content with whatever I have. I know how to live on almost nothing or with everything. I have learned the secret of living in every situation, whether it is with a full stomach or empty, with plenty or little" (Philippians 4:11-13). He emphasizes that this contentment was learned, meaning it did not arise automatically or spontaneously. Paul kept his heart open and teachable so that he could extract lessons from his life's experiences, both good and bad. Living is the only way to mature. Throughout his journey, Paul discovered that contentment was in Christ, not in his Roman citizenship, nor in his religious education, nor in his work as a tentmaker. The transformative strength is in Jesus.

One day, a sorrowful man declared: "I am bent over and racked with pain. All day long I walk around filled with grief" (Psalm 38:6). But in Christ, our life should not be a chronic lament. Remember that a Christian, even when knocked down, is not destroyed (2 Corinthians 4:9). The Scriptures teach multiple times that the children of God should walk with their heads held high, and we can highlight three reasons for this:

- Because God liberated us in the past: "I am the Lord your God, who brought you out of the land of Egypt so you would no longer be their slaves. I broke the yoke of slavery from your neck so you can walk with your heads held high" (Leviticus 26:13).
- Because God protects us in the present: "But you, O Lord, are a shield around me; you are my glory, the one who holds my head high" (Psalm 3:3).
- Because God will completely save us in the future: "So when all these things begin to happen, stand and look up, for your salvation is near!" (Luke 21:28).

Psalm 150 invites us to praise God with music and joy: "Praise him with a blast of the ram's horn; praise him with the lyre and harp! Praise him with the tambourine and dancing; praise him with strings and flutes! Praise him with a clash of cymbals; praise him with loud clanging cymbals" (Psalm 150:3-5). Biblical scholar Derek Kidner made an interesting observation about these musical instruments, stating that various aspects of Israel's life are in view here: the trumpet was used in large national and sacred gatherings (Leviticus 25:9); tambourines and dances were common in victory celebrations (Psalm 81:2;

A SENSE OF HUMOR HELPS INDIVIDUALS UNDERSTAND THEIR OWN LIMITS, BE LESS CRITICAL OF THEMSELVES, AND OPENS DOORS TO A LIGHTER, MORE INTELLIGENT LIFE.

149:3); and flutes were everyday instruments (Genesis 4:21; John 21:12; Job 30:31).[5] In other words, these instruments also point to different moments in life: solemn assemblies, trivial moments, victories, and defeats. This is how we should worship God: at all times, with all our resolve.

We are often obstinate about insignificant things. We take our personal tastes and opinions to the extreme. We are uncompromising with our political, cultural, and sporting views, and even with our whims. And often, we do not honor God in this way. We miss opportunities to worship our beloved Jesus with our resilience, tenacity, and perseverance. We give up easily, murmur instantly, and curse instead of worship. Jesus taught that even in the midst of unjust persecution, we can rejoice: "Be happy about it! Be very glad! For a great reward awaits you in heaven. And remember, the ancient prophets were persecuted in the same way" (Matthew 5:12).

Secondly, we need to *pray continually*. Continuous prayer prevents spiritual exhaustion, as it keeps the soul warmed by God's grace. The Bible encourages us to replace anxiety with prayer: "Don't worry about anything; instead, pray about everything. Tell God what you need, and thank him for all he has done" (Philippians 4:6). The anxieties of the soul and the instabilities of the world should ignite in us a greater desire for God. We saw in chapter three that Jesus maintained a life of constant prayer. He prayed in the silence of the night, in the mountains, in the deserts, and during difficult times. The Gospels record that Jesus prayed on the eve of his crucifixion. In this way, we learn the importance of going through the dramatic and painful moments of life in prayer before God. Prayer lays the foundation for peace in our hearts. Peace is often rare in the life of people who have not learned to meet with God in prayer, within their own soul.

In our prayers, we can also intercede more for other people, that is, bring others' prayer requests before God. The experienced and devout missionary Wesley L. Duewel encourages us to create prayer and intercession lists. He taught the following practical lessons:

- *Record prayer lists in a small notebook.* This notebook can serve as a prayer diary and assist in your daily time alone with God.

- *Use a portable list.* A portable list can be kept in your pocket or stored on your cell phone. Take advantage of free moments during the day to meditate in a spirit of prayer, using the names and items on the list.

- *Keep prayer lists handy.* Place them by the kitchen sink to read while washing dishes, on the bathroom mirror to intercede while shaving, and so on.

- *Use daily incidents as an unwritten prayer list.* When passing by a school, intercede for the students. When waiting in a bank line, intercede for the employees. And so on. Pray for people who call you. Pray based on news from newspapers. Pray for the people you meet throughout the day. Do not visit God occasionally; dwell in Him through prayer.[6]

Thirdly, we need to *give thanks in all circumstances*. The New Testament associates ingratitude with the essence of idolatry in ancient times (Romans 1:21) and with the marks of apostasy in the last days (2 Timothy 3:1-2). Ungrateful people struggle to recognize that life has been given to them, and can become grumpy, whining, and arrogant. In contrast, gratitude is a distinctive characteristic of those reached by the saving grace of Jesus Christ. The grateful recognize life as a blessing from God, a gift received. There is a complete reversal in perspective. In this way, we learn that gratitude changes everything. Those who constantly complain about life ruin not only their own happiness but also the happiness of others. Therefore, it is written: "Do everything without complaining and arguing" (Philippians 2:14). Gratitude operates a new way of living in us: from the inside out. What happens outside does not have the final control over our lives. Only Jesus is the Lord of our hearts.

The apostle Paul is an example of a person who underwent this regenerating experience. Before being transformed by Jesus, he considered himself righteous, was full of himself, and felt entitled to persecute and destroy those who thought differently. He was so aggressive that he was "breathing out murderous threats against the Lord's disciples" (Acts 9:1, NIV). However, after being transformed, Paul referred to himself as the worst of all sinners (1 Timothy 1:15), and said "everything else is worthless when compared with the infinite value of knowing Christ Jesus my Lord" (Philippians 3:8). Whereas before he breathed violence, now he breathes gratitude. Paul's transformation is notable: he mentions his grateful heart numerous times in his epistles (Romans 1:8; 1 Corinthians 1:4; Ephesians 1:16; Philippians1:3; Colossians 1:3; Philemon 1:4).

The work of regeneration in the lives of Christians opens up the possibility of a new attitude towards existence, a grateful stance. Indeed, everything in the Christian life is by grace, from beginning to end. As Thomas Brooks stated: "Grace turns lions into lambs, wolves into sheep, monsters into men, and men into angels."

8

Don't Comment on All the World's News

At the dawn of the 21st century, the internet connected people in an unprecedented way. Despite the undeniable benefits, this hyperconnection has brought challenges and drawbacks. In this chapter, we will address an intense challenge: cognitive overload.

We live in a world of people who are full of confused, accelerated, anxious thoughts, eager for the latest news. There is talk of "password fatigue" and "identity chaos" caused by the extensive and growing number of devices, applications, and online profiles we need to manage. While technological gadgets are a novelty, however, the anxious impetus to stay connected is not entirely new. The Bible repeatedly offers guidance for a wise and sober approach to handling numerous news sources. In Ecclesiastes, for example, we find the admonition: "Don't eavesdrop on others—you may hear your servant curse you. For you know how often you yourself have cursed others" (Ecclesiastes 7:21-22). In other words, the Scriptures teach that it is wise to live one's own life, occupy one's time with noble activities, and avoid gossiping and meddling. Creating fake digital profiles and avatars to snoop into others' lives is not prudent. In addition to the irreparable waste of time, the eavesdropper becomes vulnerable to all sorts of useless and harmful information.

The urge to comment on all subjects and news is also foolish, as the Scriptures warn: "Watch your tongue and keep your mouth shut, and you will stay out of trouble" (Proverbs 21:23). The political realm, in particular, has become characterized by incessant digital chatter. It is interesting to note that as early as 1984, the professor of legal and political theory Norberto Bobbio reflected on the possibility of information technology altering the structure of democratic-representative societies. At the time, he called this the "hypothesis of future computer-ocracy," which would include the possibility of exercising direct democracy by citizens through computerized voting. The question was: could the advancement of technology create a "computerized democracy" in which people would no longer need political representatives? Bobbio considered this scenario implausible because, judging by the number of laws passed each year, citizens would be called upon to express their vote at least once a day. Moreover, according to Bobbio, excessive participation could result in political satiety and increased electoral apathy.[2] In other words, the professor opposed the "total citizen," a derogatory term proposed by Ralf Dahrendorf to describe an individual overwhelmed by political activism, incapable of doing anything else in life.[3]

Today, social media, smartphones, and Wi-Fi connections are an integral part of the daily lives of billions of people around the world. Similarly, political participation via digital means is already a reality. We may not have the ability to vote directly on everything, but we can give our opinions on everything. Political action now takes multiple new forms: legislators using apps to consult their constituents in real time; heads of state exchanging insults on social media; digital militias using bots to destroy political reputations, and so on. Thus, the effects of new technologies are revealed to be mixed, according to common sense: there are advances, such as new possibilities of monitoring and transparency of government, but there are also setbacks, such as the sensationalization of discourse.

The advent of new media has established a short-term, everyday, and banal logic, giving the false impression that it is possible to solve complex political issues without institutional safeguards, with mere slogans and catchphrases. In fact, in our "spectacle society," there is an enormous number of people who aspire to offer daily surprises with controversies, scandals, and false dilemmas, all in search of attention. Especially in the political field, voluntarism devoid of institutional checks and balances has disastrous consequences, as revealed particularly by the totalitarian experiences of the past century. The cleansing of society starts with the acknowledgment and confrontation of reality, not with alienation and improvisation.

Numerous studies show that extreme verbosity in digital media has devastating effects on mental health.[4] The apostle Paul highlighted that excessive speaking is also harmful to spiritual life. It is interesting to note that the apostle opens and closes his first letter to Timothy with instructions about not getting into stupid arguments: "I urged you to stay there in Ephesus and stop those whose teaching is contrary to the truth. Don't let them waste their time in endless discussion of myths and spiritual pedigrees. These things only lead to meaningless speculations, which don't help people live a life of faith in God" (1 Timothy 1:3-4); "Avoid godless, foolish discussions with those who oppose you with their so-called knowledge. Some people have wandered from the faith by following such foolishness" (1 Timothy 6:20-21). Paul was uncompromising on this point.

Christians are not under the law, but under grace (Romans 6:14).[5] As free people in Christ Jesus, we are called to live with wisdom, discernment, justice, and love according to the gospel.

"TOTAL CITIZEN" IS THE DEROGATORY TERM PROPOSED BY RALF DAHRENDORF TO DESCRIBE AN INDIVIDUAL ENGULFED IN POLITICAL ACTIVISM, INCAPABLE OF DOING ANYTHING ELSE IN LIFE.

In practice, this presents specific challenges. When addressing these issues in his first letter to the Corinthians, the apostle Paul presents some basic principles. In our participation on social media, we can then ask ourselves some questions in a spirit of prayer before God:

- Is this enslaving me? *"'I am allowed to do anything'—but not everything is good for you. And even though 'I am allowed to do anything,' I must not become a slave to anything'"* (1 Corinthians 6:12). A sober approach to social media includes not being enslaved by these platforms nor by the opinions of others. Virtual addiction is already a trait of contemporary youth, with its idle and anxious behavior. In his study on the nihilism of contemporary youth, renowned philosopher and psychoanalyst Umberto Galimberti observed the "cult of the sincere" that exists on social media, as if the perpetual exposure of one's intimacy and all opinions on every subject serves as proof of sincerity and innocence.[6] Under this veneer of "sincerity" lies nothing more than someone enslaved to themselves and to the opinions of others.

- Does this edify? *"'I am allowed to do anything'—but not everything is good for you. You say, 'I am allowed to do anything'—but not everything is beneficial'"* (1 Corinthians 10:23). Are our posts useful in any way? Or are we just adding to the ranks of sin disseminators, of chaos propagators? In Scripture, the Christian is called a "minister of reconciliation" and "co-worker of God." Let no corrupt post come from our fingers. What is the usefulness of this post? Is there any value in this post, or will it simply add to the virtual trash and the overload of superfluous information on the internet? The Bible teaches that "a gentle answer deflects anger, but harsh words make tempers flare. The tongue of the wise makes knowledge appealing, but the mouth of a fool belches out foolishness" (Proverbs 15:1-4).

- Does this exalt God? *"So whether you eat or drink, or whatever you do, do it all for the glory of God"* (1 Corinthians 10:31). How can the glory of God be seen through this post? Is my motivation to glorify God or myself? On social media which is characterized by the legitimization of the selfie, the self-portrait, and posting oneself, there is the obvious and self-evident narcissistic temptation, the essence of sin: pride, self-ostentation, and alienation from God. The Christian, above all, must keep their eyes on Christ, the author and finisher of our faith. God is the one who searches and knows our hearts.
- Is this a good example? *"Don't give offense to Jews or Gentiles or the church of God. I, too, try to please everyone in everything I do. I don't just do what is best for me; I do what is best for others so that many may be saved"* (1 Corinthians 10:32-33). What testimony does this behavior communicate to people? Am I drawing people closer to God or pushing them away?

In many cases, it is important to simply disconnect from social media. Social media can become mere chewing gum for the eyes. Too much external stimulation clogs our thoughts and hinders our emotional well-being. The more connected we are, the more restless we can become.

Therefore, try to set a time every day when you completely disconnect from technology. It is important to have "zero electronics" spaces and moments: no internet, no video games, no television, no email, no digital media. Your life will not end if you "miss" other people's posts. You don't need to be a slave to technology. Avoid instantly responding to every message alert you receive on your phone. Avoid the futile habit of binge-watching TV series uninterruptedly. It's one thing to relax on vacation by watching something fun; it's quite another to become an alienated series addict.[7] Read good books, interact with people who bring you joy, practice sports, spend more time with God. Virtual reality does not replace the concrete reality of life as a whole and its communal dimension in the church. In the digital age, we must not stop using our analog selves: touching, hugging, crying, and laughing with each other. The reality of collective worship, of bread and wine shared within a human community made of flesh and blood, cannot be replaced by social media. Jesus was not digitized, nor did he die in pixels. He incarnated, lived among us, died on the cross of Calvary, and rose on the third day.

9
Nurture Patience

As God is the author of patience,
so the devil is of impatience.

TERTULLIAN[1]

Patience is the name of a plant (*rumex patientia*), of a card game, and of a virtue: enduring the unpleasantness of life without continuous irritation or exaggerated anxiety. Patience is both tolerance in the face of other people's failures and the calm waiting for some event that will change uncomfortable circumstances. Patience is not to be confused, therefore, with giving up or mere resignation. In fact, the term "patient" is also applied to a sick person undergoing medicinal treatment, awaiting recovery. Thus, patience carries the idea of enduring treatments and healing circumstances without complaint. Love is patient. Therefore, it is written: "Be patient with each other" (Ephesians 4:2). In the Bible, patience is strength. Impatience, on the other hand, only causes confusion.

In a well-known aphorism, the writer Franz Kafka stated:

There are two main human sins, from which all the others derive: impatience and indolence. It was because of impatience that they were expelled from paradise; it is because of indolence that they do not return. Yet perhaps there is only one major sin: impatience. Because of impatience they were expelled, because of impatience they do not return.[2]

Indeed, constant impatience and irritability are extremely harmful. Unfortunately, there are people with short tempers,

PATIENCE IS

STRENGTH.

who explode at random, harming themselves and others. Faced with life's problems, many simply let anger expand within them. The psalmist condemns this attitude, saying: "Stop being angry! Turn from your rage! Do not lose your temper—it only leads to harm" (Psalm 37:8).

We can mention at least four major types of damage that anger can cause in us. First, anger opens doors for us to do foolish things: "Short-tempered people do foolish things, and schemers are hated" (Proverbs14:17). Irritable people constantly say and do things they shouldn't. Anger prevents a person from seeing situations with the necessary clarity. The impulse of anger is destructive rather than constructive. The irritable burn themselves up inside and exhaust the patience of others, causing wounds to everyone.

In second place, anger is a shortcut to violence. Genesis states that "This made Cain very angry, and he looked dejected" and then he "attacked his brother, Abel, and killed him" (Genesis 4:5, 8). The majority of people convicted of murder have no criminal history. Anger is treacherous and, if not contained, can lead to all kinds of aggression. The Lord Jesus warned his disciples: harboring anger in your heart is already a murderous attitude subject to divine judgment (Matthew 5:21-22).

In the third place, anger gives opportunities to the devil. The apostle Paul was emphatic: "Don't sin by letting anger control you. Don't let the sun go down while you are still angry, for anger gives a foothold to the devil" (Ephesians 4:26-27). In other words, if we do not know how to appropriately channel our feelings of indignation, the tendency will be for them to end up overcoming us. The devil takes control when we are irritated. A popular proverb states: "Anger begins with folly, and ends with repentance."[3]

Fourth, "Human anger does not produce the righteousness God desires" (James 1:20). In other words, losing patience, even for a short time, can have devastating effects. Some people say they lose their patience but quickly regain control just a minute later. The problem is that in just one minute, the atomic bomb exploded in Hiroshima, and look at the damage it caused. No wonder the development of a stable, patient, and persevering character is highly valued in the Scriptures: "Better to be patient than powerful; better to have self-control than to conquer a city" (Proverbs 16:32). In biblical logic, the greatest demonstration of power lies in mastering oneself, not others.

The New Testament explicitly states that patience and self-control are also spiritual attributes, mentioning them as aspects of the fruit of the Spirit (Galatians 5:23). In other words, the ability to control one's impulses is one of God's graces in a person's life, a competence that flourishes in the life of someone filled with the Holy Spirit. When we are filled with the Spirit, he transforms us and governs our choices. An example of personal change in this regard is Simon Peter, a disciple of Jesus. Simon is described in the pages of the Gospels as someone impulsive, intense, and often reckless. When Jesus was washing his disciples' feet, "Peter protested, 'you will never ever wash my feet!' Jesus replied, 'Unless I wash you, you won't belong to me'" (John 13:8). "Then Simon Peter exclaimed, 'Then wash my hands and head as well, Lord, not just my feet!'" (John 13:9). It is curious how Peter changed from "you will never ever wash my feet" to "Then wash my hands and head as well." He went from one extreme to the other. Following these events, Peter's impulsiveness is also seen in his declaration, "Even if everyone else deserts you, I will never desert you" (Matthew 26:33). The end of the story is well known: before the rooster crowed, Peter denied Jesus three times. However, the Bible records Peter's profound conversion and the development of his solid, mature, patient, and persevering leadership. If even Peter's volatility was healed, there is hope for all of us.

How can we nurture patience and self-control? First, *we must not feed anger*. "Fools vent their anger, but the wise quietly hold it back" (Proverbs 29:11). Anger leads a person to speak thoughtless, senseless things that they may not even believe in. For instance, in his second book of *Rhetoric*, the philosopher Aristotle states that "emotions are all those feelings that so change men as to affect their judgements."[4]

It is crucial, therefore, to develop the ability to curb the expansive feeling of anger. There are several ways to do this. For example, a couple should know how to end a disagreement, just as friends need to moderate their emotions in a discussion. Another prudent attitude is to notice when the voice is raised in an argument. Nothing lowers a conversation more than raising one's voice uncontrollably. Hatred distorts the face—even hatred against sordidness. Yelling makes the voice hoarse—even yelling against injustice. It is also important not to respond to a tense situation while angry. We are masters of the words we keep but slaves of those we utter. Remember that spoken words are always irreversible; once said, they cannot be "unsaid." While apologies can be made and retractions issued, it is impossible to "unsay" something. Thomas Jefferson wisely said: "When angry, count ten, before you speak; if very angry, an hundred." Indeed, learning to cut off the flow of anger as soon as possible is very beneficial for anyone seeking to develop verbal and emotional control.

Second, it is necessary *to learn to live with discomfort*. "Rejoice in our confident hope. Be patient in trouble, and keep on praying" (Romans 12:12). We should not only set a limit on our anger but also crucify our rage through the total surrender of our soul to God. Our unpleasant feelings can be placed before God in prayer. Once again, we understand the importance of prayer for emotional restoration. Spending time with God reshapes our perception of situations. This is very important: living with patience implies not having immature and unrealistic expectations. Jesus explained that life on this earth will certainly bring surely bring discomfort (John 16:33). In communion with God we are spiritually strengthened. We enter the prayer room as kittens and leave as lions. Certain discomforts can be starting points for great changes:

- We can remember what is most important in our lives.
- We can discover an ungodly character trait that needs to be eliminated.
- We can learn new skills.
- We can break out of monotony.
- We can look beyond ourselves and see the needs of others.
- We can take on much greater responsibilities.

Thirdly, it is important to *forget offenses*. We live in an aggressive society, full of bitter people who vent their frustrations on each other. In our daily lives, we have to deal with hateful, angry people who are accustomed to offending others. Two biblical proverbs are very instructive in this regard: "A fool is quick-tempered, but a wise person stays calm when insulted" (Proverbs 12:16); and "Sensible people control their temper; they earn respect by overlooking wrongs" (Proverbs 19:11). It is not worth dwelling on offenses hurled by malicious people, nor creating a storm around oneself to resolve interpersonal disputes. Therefore, do not focus obsessively on suffered affronts. Stop frowning. The feeling of bravery may please our ego, but it is counterproductive in practice. Pride advises us to retaliate, but divine wisdom tells us to forgive. Revenge places us on the moral level of the malicious offender; forgiveness places us above them. Revenge is Satan's way of destroying both the innocent and the offender. The path of forgiveness is wiser in every respect.

The Bible proclaims God's willingness to forgive sins through the sacrifice of Jesus on the cross. When we are reached by God's forgiving and saving grace, we develop the ability to ignore offenses, forgive disloyal and malicious people, and move forward. Through these attitudes, we develop our faith in God and His sovereignty. King David showed great wisdom by saying in Psalm 37: "Don't worry about the wicked or envy those who do wrong. For like grass, they soon fade away. Like spring flowers, they soon wither" (Psalm 37:1-2). Instead of brooding over offenses, we should advance in promoting good: "Trust in the Lord and do good. Then you will live safely in the land and prosper" (Psalm 37:3).

Fourthly, we need to *learn to wait*. We live in an instant gratification society, where people are allergic to waiting. Everything has to be quick and immediate. In his work *On Waiting*, Harold Schweizer examined how the boredom of waiting has been accentuated by modern technology.[5] The frenzy of immediacy and the acceleration of life's pace has led to the emergence of various initiatives around the world in the mid-2000s advocating for a slower and calmer pace of life, such as "slow parents," "slow readers," and even "slow travelers." All these initiatives have been encompassed by the expression "slow movement" or "movement without haste."[6]

In the Bible, the association between patience, waiting, and faith is very strong: "Be still in the presence of the Lord, and wait patiently for him to act" (Psalm 37:7). To cultivate the virtue of patience, we need to learn that not everything in life can be done quickly. We need the patience of a oyster if we want to produce precious pearls. Just as the roots of a leafy tree silently

WE NEED THE PATIENCE OF AN OYSTER IF WE WANT TO PRODUCE PRECIOUS PEARLS.

develop in the soil, the habit of waiting strengthens our emotional skills and makes us more stable and mature individuals. We must not forget that between conception and the birth of a human being, there is a period of gestation. Patience makes us capable of nurturing life. The letter of James gives the example of the farmer: "Consider the farmers who patiently wait for the rains in the fall and in the spring. They eagerly look for the valuable harvest to ripen. You, too, must be patient" (James 5:7-8). Waiting is sometimes difficult: the doctor who is running late; the traffic jam; the slow processing of a computer; the storm that needs to calm down for us to continue our journey. But as the title of the song by my friend and songwriter Marcos Almeida says, "to wait is to walk." The ability to wait tempers actions and matures thoughts.

Last, we can reflect on examples of patience. One of the early church fathers who reflected and wrote about patience was Tertullian, the author of *On Patience*. Although this text was written in specific circumstances of Christian persecution and martyrdom, it presents three biblical examples of patience in general: God the Father, who is patient with our disobedience; Christ, who endures our offenses and saves us through His death and resurrection; and Job, who endured suffering without blaspheming against God. Tertullian followed James's advice to reflect Job's patience: "For examples of patience in suffering, dear brothers and sisters, look at the prophets who spoke in the name of the Lord. We give great honor to those who endure under suffering. For instance, you know about Job, a man of great endurance. You can see how the Lord was kind to him at the end, for the Lord is full of tenderness and mercy" (James 5:10-11).

Indeed, the book of Job is a literary and spiritual treasure. The French writer Victor Hugo is said to have remarked that

"The book of Job is perhaps the greatest masterpiece of the human mind."[7] The story of Job is challenging: he was a prosperous man in the desert, but lost everything after being attacked by Satan. He fell ill, lost his children and his properties, and became an outcast in the community. A broad public debate speculated on the causes of Job's misfortune: Was God punishing him for his sins? Yet God Himself responded to his servant, redirecting the questions to another perspective: divine sovereignty, wisdom, and mercy are above and beyond human limitations.

The struggles we face in life cannot be reduced to ready-made formulas. Job did not receive explanations about the causes of his suffering, but he received something much greater and more powerful: knowledge about who his God is. Therefore, Job said, "I had only heard about you before, but now I have seen you with my own eyes" (Job 42:5). As if that were not enough, God also restored Job's fortunes and blessed him even more in the latter part of his life than in the first.

10

Develop Meaningful Relationships

It's better to share a steak than to eat liver alone.

BUMPER STICKER ON A BRAZILIAN TRUCK

Everything in life revolves around relationships. A central biblical passage on this theme is Ecclesiastes 4:7-12. The text highlights the futility of working just to pursue wealth and possessions without meaningful connections and purpose. At some point, this lonely person will ask, "Who am I working for? Why am I giving up so much pleasure now?" (Ecclesiastes 4:8). A life without friendships is a dull, insipid and senseless life. On the other hand, "Two people are better off than one, for they can help each other succeed" (Ecclesiastes 4:9).

It was God himself who created us as relational beings. We all need an ally. Ecclesiastes presents three blessings of friendship from a concrete image: a long journey. The first blessing of friendship is support: " If one person falls, the other can reach out and help. But someone who falls alone is in real trouble" (Ecclesiastes 4:10). There are potholes, unforeseen events, and eventualities on the roads of life. There are both literal and figurative falls. When we have friends, we have support in difficult situations.

The second blessing of friendships is described as follows: "Two people lying close together can keep each other warm. But how can one be warm alone?" (Ecclesiastes 4:11). To face the challenge of cold nights, two friends can unite. Notice that in the first challenge, one friend fell and the other helped. In this second one, both face the cold together.

The third blessing of friendships is protection: "A person standing alone can be attacked and defeated, but two can stand back-to-back and conquer. Three are even better, for a triple-braided cord is not easily broken" (Ecclesiastes 4:12). In life, there are cowardly attackers, but there are also protective friends. Our love for others propels us forward.

True friendships are cultivated, not bought. There are a number of steps we can take to develop meaningful relationships. *First, we must abandon the folly of an individualistic life.* "Unfriendly people care only about themselves; they lash out at common sense" (Proverbs 18:1). We live in an exclusionary, segregated, and narcissistic society. Stories circulate on the internet of people who even "marry themselves," complete with a ceremony and all. There are people who write books and dedicate them to themselves. In this self-absorbed world, it is common to hear things like "you are my problem." Indeed, there are many false friends who, as Benjamin Franklin said, are like shadows: they accompany us while we are in the light but abandon us in the difficult, dark days.

Unfortunately, many hurt people end up losing the desire to build friendships. Yet bad company does not represent everyone. Don't let past relationship traumas hinder your present and future friendships. Don't speak ill of others or be malicious. Those who only build walls are left without horizons. Small-minded people mock others because they think it will make them feel better. Avoid gratuitous negative comments. It is impossible to sow thorns and reap flowers. Closing yourself off is not wise; human life yearns for relationships. I remember a college friend who lived alone jokingly telling me: "The downside of living alone is that it's always my turn to do the dishes."

Second, we can *invest in spending time with others*. Relationships are social investments. They grow as you make small deposits in them. Take a moment to identify which relationships make you feel renewed, accepted, and comfortable. Genuine friendships are two-way streets. Invest in spending time with those who love you. The Bible offers many examples of true friendships: David and Jonathan (1 Samuel 18:1); Elijah and Elisha (2 Kings 2:2); Priscilla, Aquila, and Paul (Romans 16:4); and the early Christians (Acts 2:42). In all these cases, the interaction between friends was essential.

Indeed, it is impossible to deepen relationships without adopting an open and active attitude. There are a number of practical steps we can take: scheduling meals together; hosting or accommodating friends; sending handwritten letters; giving gifts on special occasions; supporting them during difficult times; traveling together; attending events; going for walks; calling and setting aside time to listen. Prioritize face-to-face time, *vis-à-vis*. Technology makes it easy to send a text message and it can be very convenient, but it should not replace the embodied affection of human presence.

Make a difference in someone's life. Some people sit around complaining because they lack the creative framework to transform their indignation into a gift for others. Speak words of blessing: "Worry weighs a person down; an encouraging word cheers a person up" (Proverbs 12:25). Send a caring message, use your influence to help the afflicted, and be a part of someone else's story. The best way to gain friends is to act like one.

Third, we can *value our friends*. True friendship cannot exist between petty individuals. A true friend celebrates the achievements of others. Every victory is our victory, every struggle is our struggle. The beautiful verse from the Argentine group Onda Vaga's song "Mambeado" says it perfectly: "Sing for your friends with all your heart." I am always moved when I hear it. The true beauty of friendship lies precisely in its selflessness and goodwill. A real friend wants the best for the other person. "There are 'friends' who destroy each other, but a real friend sticks closer than a brother" (Proverbs 18:24).

According to the Bible, one of the most important marks of a true friend is their loyalty: "A friend is always loyal, and a brother is born to help in time of need" (Proverbs 17:17). In the first chapter, we saw that true friends are those who have proven that they care about you over time. These are the people who listen to your complaints without making quick and hasty judgments. After all, we should not seek only our own interests but also the interests of others (Philippians 2:3-4). You can value friends by bringing up their concerns, asking about the details of their plans, and showing respect for their dilemmas.

We live in a society where it is common to badmouth others, but the Bible teaches us differently: we should give honor to whom honor is due. Paul appropriately praised his friends in Corinth (1 Corinthians 11:2). This principle of valuing friends is so powerful that we are instructed to honor even the friends of our parents: "Never abandon a friend—either yours or your father's" (Proverbs 27:10). A friend never leaves their friend on the ground. A friend stays when everyone else disappears, stands by us in times of crisis, and comes to our rescue in the middle of the night, if necessary. King David's friends were willing to die for him, because they knew he was also willing to die for them (2 Samuel 23:15-17). Jesus said, "There is no greater love than to lay down one's life for one's friends" (John 15:13).

Fourth, *we should not be overly sensitive.* "As iron sharpens iron, so a friend sharpens a friend" (Proverbs 27:17). Those who have a good friend do not need a mirror. Charles Spurgeon said that the harsh slaps of truth are better than the kisses of betrayal. A true friend is more concerned with our growth than our vanity. They will say things that may seem unpleasant at first, but will make us sharper for life. We cannot live surrounded by self-serving flatterers. Fake compliments and friendships can distort our understanding of reality and get us into trouble. In fact, real friendships require sincerity; therefore, we cannot be hypersensitive.

A friend is someone who has earned the right to be heard, who has listened to our entire story, understood our point of view, and now should have the freedom to share their impressions. Therefore, listen and learn. When you stay quiet and give others a chance to speak, you have the opportunity to learn. When you have friends, you quickly discover that you are not the exception, that you are not the only person with problems. It is liberating and restorative to understand that life does not revolve around you. If you are repeatedly criticized in a certain area, it is worth seriously reflecting on the matter. Some people, when faced with recurring criticism, make excuses, criticize others back, or ignore what was said, creating various ways to avoid properly reflecting on the criticism they have received. It is true that we often receive unfair criticism that hurts us. It is wise to reflect sincerely on criticism, however, especially when it is recurring or comes from someone trustworthy.

When Nathan rebuked David, he told a story about an unjust man. David became indignant upon hearing the story, even saying that the man deserved to die. But Nathan's narrative was an illustration of what David himself had done: committed adultery and orchestrated the death of a loyal soldier. Nathan confronted David: "You are that man!" David then acknowledged his mistake (2 Samuel 12:1-15). It is worth noting that the ability to be frank doesn't mean telling a friend they're wrong all the time. Someone who constantly points out flaws is not a friend, they're a headache. The urge to be contrary ruins happy moments. Remember that true friendships are healthy. Strive to

HE WHO HAS

A GOOD FRIEND

DOES NOT NEED

A MIRROR.

be emotionally aware in your relationships. For example, if you feel anxious around a certain person and notice that your mood improves when you are away from them, it's time to evaluate the effect that relationship is having on your emotional health.

Above all, we must be *friends of God*. We cannot neglect the deepest foundations of our relationships. Undoubtedly, our relational and existential foundations are in God Himself. Perhaps you are looking among the branches for what only appears in the roots. Is your soul truly rooted in God? The beloved theologian J. I. Packer stated: "God relates to Christians not only as Father to child but also as Friend to friend."[1] Through Jesus, we have a new relationship with God and are healed, restored, and empowered to relate to others. You can only give what you have:

- We are accepted by God (Titus 3:7), so we can accept others.
- We are forgiven by God (Romans 8:1), so we can forgive.
- We are valued by God (1 Corinthians 7:23), so we can value others.

In Christ, therefore, we can rebuild our relationships with God and with others. Jesus Himself is the supreme example of a friend and invites us to a life of friendship with Him: "Now you are my friends, since I have told you everything the Father told me" (John 15:15).

Conclusion

What remained beyond the lightning scar?

ANA MARTINS MARQUES[1]

This world will fade away, along with everything that people crave. But the Bible teaches that whoever does what pleases God lives forever (1 John 2:17). In this work, we looked at a set of priceless biblical instructions for emotional, mental, and spiritual restoration:

- Vent, lament, and cry
- Cultivate the virtue of humility
- Create cycles of rest
- Examine your life regularly
- Take care of your body
- Maintain mental hygiene
- Celebrate, pray, and give thanks
- Don't comment on all the world's news
- Nurture patience
- Develop meaningful relationships

All these attitudes are pleasing to God and, with his help, will flourish in our lives. It is written: "For God is working in you, giving you the desire and the power to do what pleases him" (Philippians 2:13). When we truly surrender our lives to the Lord Jesus, we receive the necessary strength to live and fulfill the Father's will.

Do not doubt the power of God. What leads you to believe that your problems are so big that not even God can remove them? Reflect carefully on Jesus's invitation:

> Come to me, all of you who are weary and carry heavy burdens, and I will give you rest. Take my yoke upon you. Let me teach you, because I am humble and gentle at heart, and you will find rest for your souls. 30 For my yoke is easy to bear, and the burden I give you is light.
>
> Matthew 11:28-30

Jesus uses the image of a load-bearing animal, like an ox or a horse, that has an excessively heavy yoke and load. This animal has three characteristics: it is (1) tired, (2) overloaded, and (3) disoriented. If you feel this way, it is important to recognize and admit your situation. There is no point in denying the obvious. What's the point of saying "I'm fine" if your eyelids are twitching from stress? Jesus knows you completely. He knows how exhausted you may be.

His invitation is very direct: "Come to me." Jesus does not say, "Go to a worship service," or "Go to your pastor." Instead, he says, "Come to me." He calls us directly to Himself. Jesus Himself is our true need. He is not a dead-end alley, but the way to a new life. Thus, it is necessary for us to repent of our sins and believe in the gospel of Jesus. At the cross, the struggle ends. At the cross, there is peace.

His promise is very direct: "and you will find rest for your souls." The problem at hand is not simply physical or psychological, but above all spiritual. In Christ, God reveals who He is and what He intends for humanity. Only in Christ are we forgiven and can receive a gentle yoke and a light burden. In Him, we are redirected to a new way of living. In Christ, we receive a new life with new interests, new standards, a new sense of security, a new strength to face frustrations, a peace that surpasses all understanding.

My prayer is that you may be restored, guided by Jesus into a blessed life of humility and meekness.

Acknowledgements

I would like to thank my wife, Natalia, for her love and affectionate support at every stage of the development of this book. Thank you, Natalia, for being so kind to me. Without you I would never have been able to write this book, nor would I have had the courage to move forward in difficult times. Our family is my treasure on this earth. Your friendship is the best part of my life. I am grateful to my daughter, Maria, for being so helpful and loving. I love you so much. Keep growing full of life and in the fear of the Lord.

I express my deepest gratitude to my parents, Elienos and Esmeralda, who from a very young age instilled in me many of the teachings I have transcribed in this book. I am also grateful to my in-laws, Roberto and Dirce, who have become like parents to me. I cherish the love and support of my entire family.

I thank my friends who are closer than brothers, Teófilo Hayashi, Gustavo Paiva, Dênio Lara Jr., Gustavo Buffara, Daniela Linhares, Fred Arrais, and William Douglas, for their availability and companionship in the production of this work. I thank Bishops Robson and Lúcia Rodovalho, Priscila and Lucas

Cunha, Lia and João, Samuel, and the entire Sara Nossa Terra family. You are also my family.

I especially thank my friends at Editora Mundo Cristão, Mark Carpenter, Renato Fleischner, Silvia Justino, Daniel Faria, Ricardo Dinapoli, Selmi Aquino, and the entire team. You are a blessing in my life.

Notes

Introduction

[1] Alison J. Gray and Christopher C.H. Cook, "Christianity and Mental Health," *Oxford University Press Academic*, July 1, 2021, https://academic.oup.com/book/35499/chapter-abstract/304497769?redirectedFrom=fulltext.

1. Vent, Lament, Cry

[1] Manoel de Barros and Idra Novey, *Birds for a demolition: Poems* (Pittsburgh: Carnegie Mellon University Press, 2010), p. 59.

[2] J. W. Pennebaker, J. K. Kiecolt-Glaser e R. Glaser, "Disclosure of traumas and immune function: Health implications for psychotherapy," *Journal of Consulting and Clinical Psychology*, vol. 56, nº 2, 1988, p. 239-245.

[3] Serife Tekin, "Ethical issues surrounding artificial intelligence technologies in mental health psychotherapy chatbots," in: Gregory J. Robson e Jonathan Y. Tsou (eds.), *Technology Ethics: A Philosophical Introduction and Readings* (New York & London: Routledge, 2023), p. 152-159.

[4] June Dickie "Practising Healthy Theology in the Local Church: Lamenting with Those in Pain and Restoring Hope". *Stellenbosch Theological Journal*, vol. 7 n. 1, 2021.

[5] For the contrast between the ideal of a noble death and the Christian perspective on death, see Adela Yarbro Collins, "From Noble Death to Crucified Messiah," *New Testament Studies*, vol. 40, no. 4, October 1994, p. 481-503; for the contrast between the deaths of Socrates and Jesus, see Oscar Cullmann, "Immortality of the soul or resurrection of the dead: The witness of the New Testament," in: Krister Stendahl (ed.), *Immortality and Resurrection: Death in the Western World; Two Conflicting Currents of Thought* (New York: Macmillan, 1965), p. 9-53.

[6] Plato, *Phaedo*, translated by David Gallop, 1st ed. (Oxford University Press, 2009).

[7] Origen, "Homilies on Luke 38", in: *Selections from Commentaries and Homilies of Origen* (London: Society for the Promotion of Christian Knowledge, 1929), p. 165.

[8] In 1955, in the vicinity of Jerusalem, on the Mount of Olives, the Franciscans erected a tear-shaped chapel called *Dominus Flevit*, which is the Latin expression for "the Lord wept." See P. B. Bagatti, J. T. Milik, *Gli Scavi del "Dominus Flevit" – Parte I – La necropoli del periodo romano* (Gerusalemme: Tipografia dei PP. Francescani, 1958).

[9] In John 11:35 the term is *edakrysen*; in Luke 19:41, *eklausen*.

[10] C. V. Bellieni, "Meaning and Importance of Weeping", *New Ideas in Psychology*, 47, 2017, p. 72-76.

[11] R. R. Cornelius, "Crying and catharsis", in: Vingerhoets A. J. J. M., Cornelius R. R. (eds.), *Adult Crying: A Biopsychosocial Approach*, p. 199-212.

[12] R. R. Provine, K. A. Krosnowski, and N. W. Brocato, "Tearing: breakthrough in human emotional signaling", *Evolutionary Psychology*, vol. 7, n° 1, 2009, p. 52-56.

2. Cultivate the Virtue of Humility

[1] François Rochefoucauld, E. H. Blackmore, A. M. Blackmore, and Francine Giguère, *Collected Maxims and Other Reflections* (Oxford: Oxford University Press, 2008), pp. 186-187.

[2] Paulo Leminski, "bem no fundo," in: *Distraídos Venceremos* (São Paulo: Companhia das Letras, 2017), p. 35 (English translation mine).

[3] The Hebrew term is *zadon*, also used, for example, in Proverbs 13:10 and 21:24. *Zadon* indicates the arrogance manifested in people who are intemperate and abusive in words and actions. The root of *zadon* is *zeyd* ("to boil"). When heat is applied to water, it boils. It was from this process that the Hebrews communicated their understanding of pride. The term *zeyd* appears in Genesis 25:29 to refer to the stew prepared by Jacob for his brother Esau; see Stephen B. Dawes, "Walking humbly: Micah 6:8 revisited," *Scottish Journal of Theology*, vol. 41, no. 3, 1988, p. 333; Eugene E. Carpenter, et al., *Holman Treasury of Key Bible Words: 200 Greek and 200 Hebrew Words Defined and Explained* (Nashville, TN: Broadman & Holman Publishers, 2000), p. 140.

[4] R. F. Baumeister, "Threatened egotism, narcissism, self-esteem, and direct and displaced aggression: Does self-love or self-hate lead to violence?" *Journal of Personality and Social Psychology*, vol. 75, n° 1, 1998, p. 219-229.

[5] St. Augustine, "Psalm 31.2.18", *Comentário aos Salmos (Enarrationes in psalmos: Salmos 1—50* (São Paulo: Paulus, 1997), p. 225.

[6] Debora W. Ruddy mentions Clement of Alexandria, Origen, Gregory of Nyssa, Basil, Ambrose, and John Chrysostom as examples of Patristic authors who emphasized humility as a cardinal Christian virtue; see "The humble God: Healer, mediator, and sacrifice," *Logos: A Journal of Catholic Thought and Culture*, vol. 7, no. 3, 2004, p. 87-108; Pierre Adnès, "Humilité," in: *Dictionnaire de Spiritualité, Ascétique et Mystique*, vol. VII (Paris: Beauchesne, 1969), p. 1136-1187.

[7] St. Augustine, "Salmo 31.2.18", p. 225.

[8] Roderich Barth, "The rationality of humility," *European Journal for Philosophy of Religion*, vol. 6, n° 3, 2014, p. 101-116.

[9] Professor Kent Dunnington asserts that, in contemporary philosophy, there are attempts to emancipate the virtue of humility from its Christian theological roots. Three main notions of humility are discussed in the theoretical framework: (i) the first notion

understands humility as proper self-esteem, that is, the humble person is one who has an accurate estimate of their worth, abilities, achievements, status, and rights, and is particularly resistant to overestimating these aspects; (ii) the second notion understands humility as proper unselfishness, that is, the humble person is one who cares very little about their own worth, abilities, achievements, status, or rights, as they are more concerned with other things; (iii) the third notion understands humility as proper acknowledgment of possessing limitations, that is, the humble person owns their limitations: they take them seriously, are troubled by having them, do everything possible to rid themselves of them, but accept them and do their best to control and minimize their negative effects; see *Humility, Pride, and Christian Virtue Theory* (Oxford, UK: Oxford University Press, 2019).

[10] June Price Tangney, "Humility: Theoretical Perspectives, empirical findings and directions for future research," *Journal of Social and Clinical Psychology*, vol. 19, n° 1, 2000, p. 70-82.

[11] François Rochefoucauld, in: E. H. Blackmore, A. M. Blackmore, and Francine Giguère. *Collected Maxims and Other Reflections* (Oxford: Oxford University Press, 2008), p. 99.

3. Create Cycles of Rest

[1] Billy Graham, "10 Quotes from Billy Graham on the Sabbath - the Billy Graham Library Blog," Billy Graham Evangelistic Society, April 15, 2020, https://billygrahamlibrary.org/blog-10-quotes-from-billy-graham-on-sabbath/.

[2] Ministério da Saúde, "Você já teve insônia? Saiba que 72% dos brasileiros sofrem com alterações no sono", March 17, 2023, https://www.gov.br/saude/pt-br/assuntos/noticias/2023/marco/voce-ja-teve-insonia-saiba-que-72-dos-brasileiros-sofrem- com-alteracoes-no-sono.

[3] Ministério da Saúde, "Síndrome de Burnout", Saúde de A a Z, <https://www.gov.br/saude/pt-br/assuntos/saude-de-a-a-z/s/sindrome-de-burnout>.

[4] World Health Organization, "Burn-out an 'occupational phenomenon': International Classification of Diseases," 28 May 2019, https://www.who.int/news/item/28-05-2019-burn-out-an-occupational-phenomenon-international-classification-of-diseases.

[5] Gunnar Aronsson, et al., "A systematic review including meta-analysis of work environment and burnout symptoms," *BMC Public Health*, vol. 17, 2017, p. 264.

[6] Billy Graham, *Wisdom for Each Day* (Nashville, TN: Thomas Nelson, 2008), p. 315.

[7] D. C. Bass, *Receiving the Day: Christian Practices for Opening the Gift of Time* (San Francisco, CA: Jossey-Bass), p. 5.

[8] Matthew Walker, *Why We Sleep: The New Science of Sleep and Dreams* (London: Penguin, 2018).

[9] Andrew Bishop, *Theosomnia: A Christian Theology of Sleep* (London: Jessica Kingsley Publishers, 2018), p. 64.

4. Examine Your Life Regularly

[1] Søren Kierkegaard, *For Self-Examination and Judge for Yourselves!*, translated by Walter Lowrie (Princeton: Princeton University Press, 2019), p. 50.

[2] For an excellent introductory scientific study regarding self-deception and biased optimism, see Anneli Jefferson, Lisa Bortolotti, and Bojana Kuzmanovic, "What is unrealistic optimism?", *Consciousness and Cognition*, vol. 50, 2017, p. 3-11.

[3] For a compilation of thoughts from the Scottish preacher Robert M. M'Cheyne (1813-1843), see Andrew A. Bonar, *Memoir and Remains of R.M. M'Cheyne* (Edinburgh: Banner of Truth, 1966).

[4] Shoshana Zuboff, *The Age of Surveillance Capitalism: The Fight for a Human Future at the New Frontier of Power* (New York: PublicAffairs, 2020), p. 262.

[5] Deborah Lupton, *The Quantified Self: A Sociology of Self-Trecking* (Cambridge: Polity, 2016).

⁶Yasmin Anwar, "Emoji Fans Take Heart: Scientists Pinpoint 27 States of Emotion," *Berkeley News*, May 21, 2024, https://news.berkeley.edu/2017/09/06/27-emotions/.

⁷Fernando Pessoa, *The Book of Disquiet*, edited and translated by Richard Zenith (London: Penguin Books, 2002).

5. Take Care of Your Body

¹Clarice Lispector, *Água viva*, edited by Benjamin Moser and translated by Stefan Tobler (New York: New Directions, 2012), p. 29.

²Norman Wirzba, *Food and faith: A theology of eating* (Cambridge, UK: Cambridge University Press, 2011), p. 2.

³For a Christian theological approach to food, see Angel F. Méndez Montoya, *Theology of Food: Eating and the Eucharist* (Oxford: Wiley-Blackwell, 2009), p. IX.

⁴In 1 Corinthians 10:23-33, the Apostle Paul teaches about the Christian attitude towards food sacrificed to idols, emphasizing that the mark of maturity is the ability to balance freedom with responsibility. All things are lawful, but we must ask ourselves: will they promote freedom or enslavement? (1 Cor 6:12); will they be a stumbling block or a support? (1 Cor 8:13); will they build up or destroy my life? (1 Cor 10:23); will they just be for my own pleasure or will they glorify God? (1 Cor 10:31); will they contribute to the testimony of the gospel or drive people away from Christ? (1 Cor 10:33).

⁵Becky Lehman, *Less of Me: A 30-Day Devotional for Your Weight Loss Journey* (Independently published, 2019).

⁶Angel F. Méndez Montoya, *The Theology of Food: Eating and the Eucharist* (Hoboken, NJ: Wiley-Blackwell, 2009), p. 46.

⁷World Health Organization, "Obesity and overweight," March 1st, 2024, https://www.who.int/news-room/fact-sheets/detail/obesity-and-overweight.

⁸Sanford Health, "Sitting is the new smoking: 'Truly a silent killer,'" February 9, 2023, https://news.sanfordhealth.org/heart/sitting-is-the-new-smoking-truly-a-silent-killer/.

[9] Victor Pfitzner's scholarly approach has become a reference of the sports metaphors in Pauline writings. Pfitzner highlighted how Paul used the theme of athletics in an innovative way, deviating from the Stoic thought of his time. See Victor J. Pfitzner, *Paul and the Agon Motif* (Leiden: Brill, 1967).

[10] See *agōni* in 1 Thessalonians 2:2; *stephanos* and *emprosthen* in 1 Thessalonians 2:19 and Philippians 4:1; *sunagōnisasthai* in Romans 15:30; *sunēthlesan* in Philippians 4:3; *katabrabeuetō* in Colossians 2:18; *brabeuetō* in Colossians 3:15; and *theatron* in 1Corinthians 4:9.

6. Maintain Mental Hygiene

[1] Eugene S. Paykel, "Basic concepts of depression", *Dialogues in Clinical Neuroscience*, vol. 10, n° 3, 2008, p. 279-289.

[2] John Stott, *Issues Facing Christians Today*, 4ª ed. (Grand Rapids, MI: Zondervan, 2006), p. 60.

[3] Saundra Dalton-Smith, *Sacred Rest* (New York: Faith Words, 2017), p. 54.

[4] Svetlava Boym, *The Future of Nostalgia* (New York: Basic Books, 2001), p. xvi.

7. Celebrate, Pray, and Give Thanks

[1] Luiz Miguel Duarte, *Cultive o bom humor: 18 indicações práticas* (São Paulo: Paulus, 2001), p. 10.

[2] Elben M. Lenz César, *Práticas devocionais* (Viçosa, MG: Ultimato), p. 145.

[3] Beatrice Marovich, "The Powerful Authority of Cute Animals", *Atlantic*, May 14, 2024, https://www.theatlantic.com/technology/archive/2014/05/the-beckoning-cat/362108/.

[4] Amos Oz, *How to Cure a Fanatic* (London: Vintage, 2012), p. 74.

[5] Derek Kidner, *Psalms 73-150* (Downers Grove, IL: Intervarsity Press, 2014), p. 529.

[6] Wesley L. Duewel, *Touch the World Through Prayer* (Grand Rapids, MI: Zondervan, 1986), p. 246-249.

8. Don't Comment on All the World's News

[1] Jean-Paul Jacob, cited in Sandra Carvalho (ed.), *1001 frases: As tiradas mais divertidas, invocadas, inteligentes e provocantes do mundo da tecnologia e da vida moderna* (São Paulo: Abril, 2003), p. 66.

[2] Norberto Bobbio, *The Future of Democracy: A Defence of the rules of the game*, edited by Richard Bellamy and translated by Robert Griffin (University of Minnesota Press, 1987), p. 38.

[3] Ralf Dahrendorf, *Il cittadino totale* (Torino: Centro di ricerca e di documentazione Luigi Einaudi, 1977), p. 35-59.

[4] E. Boers, et al., "Association of screen time and depression in adolescence", *JAMA Pediatrics*, vol. 173, n° 9, julho de 2019, p. 853-859.

[5] "Certainly, freedom from the law does not mean that the principles of righteousness revealed in the Old Testament Law have been invalidated. It does not mean that the Ten Commandments no longer apply to our lives today. It does not mean that we can subordinate God's holy standards to our personal preferences. And it obviously does not mean that we are free from any moral requirements. What does Christian freedom mean? It means that Christians are not bound to observe the rituals of the Old Testament. We do not have to sacrifice animals, observe ceremonial cleanliness laws, or celebrate all the new moons, feasts, and sacrifices. We do not follow the dietary laws given to Israel through Moses. We are free from all that. [...] our spiritual lives are governed not just by a code of laws, but by the grace of God, which works in us to fulfill the righteous requirements of the law (Romans 8:4). Grace teaches us to deny ungodliness and worldly desires and to live sensibly, righteously, and godly (Titus 2:12)." John MacArthur, *Com vergonha do evangelho: Quando a igreja se torna como o mundo* (São José dos Campos, SP: Fiel, 2009), p. 104.

[6] Umberto Galimberti, *L'ospite inquietante: Il nichilismo e i giovani* (Milan: Feltrinelli Editore, 2016).

[7] Romain Blondeau, *Netflix, l'aliénation en série* (Paris: Édition du Seuil, 2022).

9. Nurture Patience

[1] Tertullian, "On Patience," Chapter V, The Catholic Library Project, accessed May 15, 2024, https://catholiclibrary.org/library/view?docId=%2FSynchronized-EN%2Fanf.000081.Tertullian.OnPatience.html%3Bchunk.id.

[2] E. Kaiser & E. Wilkins, trans., *Kafka's Zurau Aphorisms - Michael Cisco* (Glossator, n.d.), https://glossator.org/wp-content/uploads/2013/11/g8-cisco2.pdf.

[3] Henry G. Bohn, *A Hand-book of Proverbs* (London: G. Bell & Sons, 1875), p. 314.

[4] Aristotle, *Rhetoric*, edited by W. D. Ross, translated by R. Rhys Roberts (Cosimo Classics, 2010), p. 60.

[5] Harold Schweizer, *On Waiting* (London: Routledge, 2008), p. 8.

[6] Carl Horoné, *In Praise of Slow: How a Worldwide Movement is Challenging the Cult of Speed* (London: Orion, 2010).

[7] Victor Hugo, cited in Henry Hampton Halley, *Pocket Bible Handbook* (Chicago: Henry H. Halley, 1946), p. 232.

10. Develop Meaningful Relationships

[1] J. I. Packer, *Concise Theology: A Guide to Historic Christian Beliefs* (Carol Stream, IL: Tyndale House, 2021), p. 186.

Conclusion

[1] Ana Martins Marques, "Relâmpagos", *Risque esta palavra* (São Paulo: Companhia das Letras, 2021), p. 28.

About the Author

David Lago has been a Baptist pastor since 2006, and currently serves as chaplain at the First Baptist Church of São Paulo. He is a professor at the São Paulo Baptist Theological College and at Armando Alvares Penteado Foundation (FAAP), as well as a research coordinator at the Laboratory of Politics, Behavior, and Media (LABÔ-PUC/SP). He is a PhD candidate in Philosophy and Theory of Law (USP), holds a master's degree in Theory of Law, and a bachelor's degree in Law (PUC-MG). He is also the host of the program "Futuro Imediato" (Immediate Future) on Univesp/ TV Cultura, an ambassador for both World Vision and the Mission in Support of the Suffering Church, as well as a board member of of the Brazilian Christian Evangelical Alliance. He is a best-selling author. Editora Mundo Cristão has also published his *Brasil polifônico*, *Ame o seu próximo* and *Formigas* (in partnership with William Douglas). He is married to Natália and father of Maria.

Reflections

Reflections

Reflections

Reflections

Reflections